Helion & Company Limited
Unit 8 Amherst Business Centre
Budbrooke Road
Warwick
CV34 5WE
England
Tel. 01926 499 619
Email: info@helion.co.uk
Website: www.helion.co.uk
Twitter: @helionbooks
Visit our blog http://blog.helion.co.uk/

Designed & typeset by Farr out Publications, Wokingham, Berkshire
Cover design by Farr out Publications, Wokingham, Berkshire

ISBN 978-1-913336-26-4

British Library Cataloguing-in-Publication Data
A catalogue record for this book is available from the British Library

CONTENTS

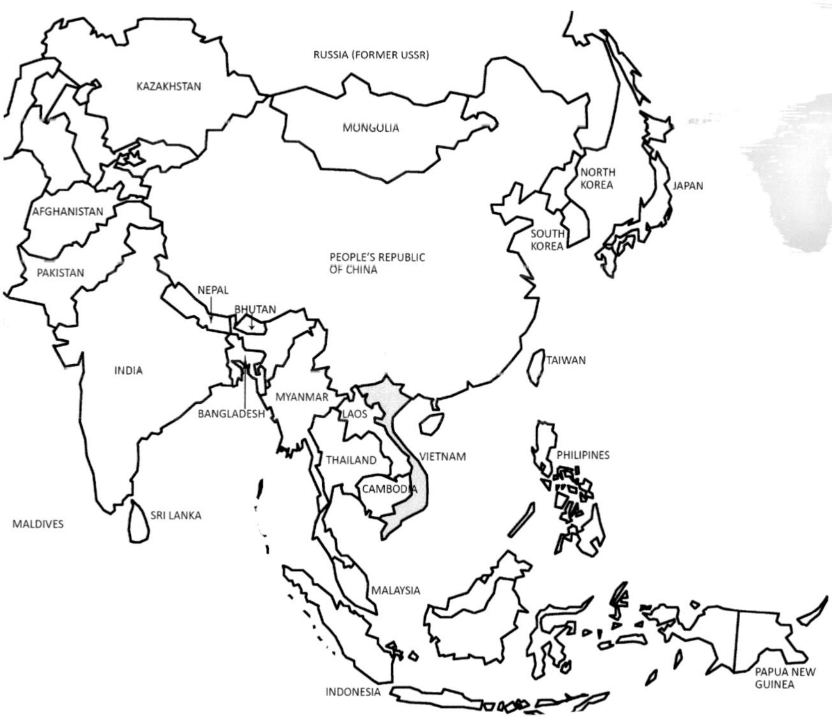

Note: In order to simplify the use of this book, all names, locations and geographic designations are as provided in *The Times World Atlas*, or other traditionally accepted major sources of reference, as of the time of described events.

ABBREVIATIONS

ARVN	Army of the Republic of Vietnam
CIDG	Civilian Irregular Defense Groups
CTZ	Corps Tactical Zone
DMZ	Demilitarised Zone
DRV	Democratic Republic of Vietnam
FAC	Forward Air Controller
FWMAF	Free World Military Assistance Forces
HHSB	Headquarters and Headquarters Service Battery
HHT	Headquarters and Headquarters Troop
MAAGV	Military Advisory and Assistance Group Vietnam
MACOV	Mechanized and Combat Operation in Vietnam
MEDCAP	Medical Civic Action Program
MSFC	Mobile Strike Force Command
NVA	North Vietnamese Army
OIDP	Overseas Internal Defense Policy
PACOM	Pacific Command
PAVN	People's Army of Vietnam
PLAF	People's Liberation Armed Forces
PROVN	Provisional Report on Vietnam
ROAD	Reorganisation Objective Army Division
RVN	Republic of Vietnam
VC	Viet Cong
VNAF	Vietnamese Air Force

INTRODUCTION

On 3 November 1966, C Company, 1-27th Infantry, the Wolfhounds, landed in an unnamed clearing north of Saigon, in what was supposed to be a routine search and destroy operation. By the evening of the same day, its company commander and company sergeant had been killed, and the battalion commander, a young major on the lieutenant colonel promotion list, Guy S. Meloy, had been wounded. In the next two days, Major Meloy and his troops would fight to a standstill the whole 101st Regiment, People's Army of Vietnam. That was the first notable act of the first multi-division operation the US Army performed in Vietnam. It saw savage fighting, mechanized charges and B-52 strikes. It also saw a brigadier general practically removed from command. It was the forerunner of General William Westmoreland's year of the offensive. But it is also a largely forgotten and misremembered battle.

The genesis of this book can be traced back to the faraway fall of 2010. I was a graduate teaching assistant at King's College London, sitting in class and discussing with students their historical analysis for their proposed conflict simulations. One student had selected as his topic the whole Vietnam War. At the same time, I was researching and writing my own PhD on American COIN doctrine and strategic culture during the Vietnam War. In the historical analysis, the student made a comment that puzzled me. He claimed that Operation ATTLEBORO did not result in significant battles. I could spend hours waxing about the laziness and lack of preparation of young students or their overreliance on Wikipedia, but that case was not one of them. The student was merely quoting a supposed reputable source, a volume produced by the US Army Center for Military History, *American Military History*. It was not his fault. The issue was and still is more complex. The source he used was misleading.

He argued that combat occurred most often at the platoon and company levels, and frequently at night. As the number of American troops increased, he said the 9th PLAF Division shied away, withdrawing across the Cambodian border.[1]

The student's source painted a completely different picture from John McGarrigle's *Combat Operations: Taking the Offensive*, the second volume of the official US Army history of the war that I had read during the preceding summer. McGarrigle's version was extensively based on battalion reports and provided detailed battle descriptions. Far from running away, the 9th PLAF Division had actively sought contact in regimental-size formations in several instances.

Fast forwarding several years, I inherited a counterinsurgency module from another teacher. The lecture on Vietnam, titled 'Firepower vs Willpower', was something that an uncharitable observer could have called an asinine rehash of myths and popular misconception. I retitled it 'Firepower vs Firepower', a much more accurate representation of the conflict.

These two examples are not isolated. In 2003, Max Boot wrote, "The biggest error the armed forces made in Vietnam was trying to fight a guerrilla foe the same way they had fought the *Wehrmacht*."[2] That a supposed serious historian ended up writing this speaks volumes on the issue. Dale Andrade, from the US Army Center of Military History, regrets that "the [US] Army's embrace of the interpretations put forth by Sorley and Nagl comes in spite of its own official history, which provides a balanced and detailed account of the war".[3] Our understanding of the Vietnam War has been largely dominated by caricatures. These caricatures dominate not just Hollywood, popular historians or 'strategic thinkers' with personal agendas, but have seeped deeply even into academic circles. What is surprising is that consensus is built despite detailed analysis and a wealth of primary and secondary sources readily available. Wars in Afghanistan, Iraq and Syria have prompted more research work on the conflict in Vietnam. I still remember when I was discussing my own research proposal back in 2008, my potential supervisor told me that Vietnam would have been useful considering the current messes around the world.

Renewed professional interest prompted the US Army to finally embark on completing its own official history of the conflict. The third volume of the combat operations series, covering 1967 and 1968, was released in 2018. Researchers now have access to a balanced, detailed and well-documented history of the US Army combat operations from 1965–68. More volumes are in preparation. Not only are official histories belatedly appearing, but the process of digitisation of records is allowing even lazy or bankrupted researchers to access primary sources from the comfort of their desks. Of course, renewed interest had graced bookshelves with a considerable amount of asinine rehashes, but plenty of excellent works have also come out. Not only American operations have been explored, but there are now several works trying to compare American and Democratic Republic of Vietnam records. Warren Wilkins's *Grab their Belts to Fight Them* is an excellent attempt to do just that.

We have reached the point that the 'orthodox consensus' is maintained in the face of reality. Explained in a different way, there is a disconnection between detailed analysis and the 'broad brush' works that, for a long series of deplorable reasons, tend to dominate the scene. Uncharitable observers would conclude that plenty of writers and academics are just too lazy to read new books and challenge their own preconceptions.

Until recently, the III Corps Tactical Zone (CTZ) has been largely ignored by historians, the focus having been the Battle of Hue in early 1968, the DMZ (the Demilitarised Zone separating North and South Vietnam) or the Central Highlands, scene of much heavy fighting. To a certain extent, formations like the 1st Cavalry Division and the US Marine Corps (USMC) have grabbed the headlines more than the bulk of the US Army. Even the late William Nolan, one of the most prolific authors covering the Vietnam War, had largely ignored the III CTZ and the period 1965–66. It is possible that the impression that the war there was just a series of relatively uneventful sweeps and patrols contributed to this dearth of books. Yet the war there was far from being fought by groups of peasants dressed in black pyjamas equipped with old rifles, taking pot-shots at American infantrymen. Hanoi's B-2 Front comprised three infantry divisions and a plethora of additional units that were not afraid of engaging the US Army or the South Vietnamese Army. On the contrary, these units more often than not actively sought prolonged contact in regiment-size formations. Until 1967 and Westmoreland's largest offensive, Operation JUNCTION CITY, the war north of Saigon was as bloody as that fought by the Marines south of the DMZ. It was also a war that had nothing to compare with clashes in the Second World War or in Korea.

This book takes an in-depth look at what happened north of Saigon between November 1965 and December 1966. To chronicle that war – a war fought primarily by the 1st Infantry Division (the Big Red One) and the 9th Division of the People's Liberation Armed Forces – I will not limit myself just to Operation ATTLEBORO, but will set the scene looking at the constant engagements between these two formations between November 1965 and the end of ATTLEBORO. I am not overly concerned about the politics of the war or the home fronts in Hanoi, Washington and Saigon. I am concerning myself with military operations waged in the so-called 'Saigon Corridor', the area between Saigon and the Cambodian border. The purpose of this book is to dispel the myth that battles in Vietnam were rare and small. They were relatively frequent and certainly big. There were no Kursks in Vietnam – and even that is a misnomer; just look at the geographical size of the battle of Kursk – but plenty of Hill 112s and Carentans.

My intention is to provide a balanced view of the battles in a particular time and place. However, I also reckon that this is impossible. All authors are biased to some extent and in some way. I make no denial of that, and my judgement of several command decisions, and several characters introduced in these pages, clearly reflect my own opinions. Operational analysis and discussion of command decisions are all my own. On the other hand, I have presented facts and numbers based on research. The bulk of the information in this book is derived from official after-action reports by US units. Where possible, PLAF sources have also been used to compare data. The latter came in two broad categories: post-war histories, usually made available to international readers by translations authored by Merle Pribbenow, and translated captured documents. The second category is available thanks to the Virtual Vietnam Archive maintained by the Texas Tech Institute. Even if the reader disagrees with my conclusions, the information presented here should be useful. I strongly hope that, my own bias notwithstanding, the reader will find my chronicling of these battles helpful and my analysis not too unbalanced.

A final note on naming conventions, acronyms and all those little things that usually abound in military history book, and that always puzzles readers. I have decided to use accurate designation as much as possible. Despite the fact that the North Vietnamese Army is usually called the NVA in the English-speaking world, this was just a US acronym. Translated into English, its name was and still is the People's Army of Vietnam, or PAVN, whereas the NVA was the *Nationale Volks Armee*, the army of East Germany. For the most part PAVN will be used throughout this book. The same is true, with some exceptions, for the Viet Cong; National Liberation Front (NLF) and People's Liberation Armed Forces (PLAF) will be used, except when referring to US Army sources, where Viet Cong or VC will be used. This exception is often due to the fact that US Army writing of the period did not make any difference between the two. For example, enemy losses during ATTLEBORO, when both PLAF and PAVN units were engaged, are just reported as VC. North Vietnam will be sometimes abbreviated as DRV, for the Democratic Republic of Vietnam, its official name. Hopefully this will not cause the readers undue confusion. The last warning is about South Vietnamese acronyms. South Vietnam's official name was the Republic of Vietnam, RVN, while its government was abbreviated as GVN. A glossary is provided for handy reference.

I sincerely hope that this book will help in the remembering of the hard-fought engagements that characterised not only Operation ATTLEBORO, but the first year of US Army operations in the Saigon area.

1
TAKING THE OFFENSIVE

When Major Guy Meloy's troops jumped out from their 'slicks' – the nickname for Huey transport helicopters – on 3 November 1966, walking toward the first major engagement of ATTLEBORO, the so-called 'American War' was already more than 12 months old. The first real American battle, Operation STARLITE, had been fought in August 1965. The war would run its course for many more years. Yet war and Vietnam had a long association.

The land that today we call the People's Republic of Vietnam has seen plenty of wars and devastation for centuries, if not millennia. Tribes, nations, kingdoms and empires have risen and fallen for centuries. Powerful neighbours, from the Khmer to several Chinese imperial dynasties, descended on it to prey, ravage and colonise. The Chinese, especially the Ming and Qing dynasties, had left a deep cultural impression on the country. Even if their armies had been forced to withdrawn, Chinese culture had remained. After the Chinese came the French, with their own agenda and culture. Even if the only Frenchmen who really profited from their colonial empire in South East Asia had probably been those involved in the straw hat industry, Paris left behind the Catholic religion and bits of French culture and language. Indochina was a land of deep history. Nevertheless, the specific country that Meloy's young soldiers were defending was relatively young too.

The Republic of Vietnam (RVN) had been officially proclaimed in October 1955 from the ashes of what once had been the *Union Française,* the French Union. After the French defeat, and Viet Minh pyrrhic victory, at Dien Bien Phu and the subsequent Geneva Accords, the border had been adjusted. A North and South Vietnam were created. As artificial as that division was, it was no more artificial than the idea of a unified Vietnam. What we call Vietnam had always been divided. The 'unification' had been achieved mere decades before the French came, and with French help. Yet that did not stop people from dreaming of a new empire on these lands. The northern portion, under the communist leadership of Ho Chi Minh, was soon to descend in a spiral of terror, revolts and retaliatory massacres; the southern part had been entrusted to an uneasy coalition of the lazy Emperor Bao Dai, the strong-willed Prime Minister Ngo Dinh Diem and their French protectors.

Saigon's fragile coalition was bound to fall quickly. Diem, a strong, anti-communist and authoritarian Vietnamese nationalist, had no time for Paris or the Riviera-loving Bao Dai. Diem had opposed both in his life. Ironically, he owed his position to French pressure on Bao Dai to appoint someone with strong nationalist credentials. The pressure had not been a purely French initiative. In his exile from Vietnam in the early 1950s, he had cultivated links with the United States. Once in power, Diem got rid of Bao Dai – still happily ensconced in southern France – and the whole French tutelage. Politicians, journalists, historians and assorted pundits have presented multiple, inconsistent and often completely inaccurate portrayals of Ngo Dinh Diem, frequently according to their own agenda. Certainly, saying that he was a complicated character was as much a simplification at the time as it is now. One thing is clear from documentary evidence: he was a committed nationalist who was firm in his vision of a strong and independent Vietnam, even if limited to the southern half. He was no proxy of anyone, especially the French. He was also a realist, realising that an independent Vietnam still needed friends; powerful friends. For the Catholic and staunchly anti-communist Diem, the only possible such friend was the United States. After a referendum deposed Bao Dai and proclaimed the Republic of Vietnam, with Diem as president, the first order of business was getting rid of the French garrison and its commander, General Paul Ely. The second order of business was establishing a functioning state. However, doing the former was much easier than the latter.

Despite Diem's friendships in the United States, Eisenhower's administration did not support him, and nor did the first US ambassador to South Vietnam, retired US Army veteran General Joseph Lawton Collins. Fresh from his mismanagement of the US Army on the eve of the Korean War, Collins wrote off the South Vietnamese president at his first crisis, only to be proven wrong when Diem triumphed over the three powerful sects that had practically run large areas of South Vietnam and controlled much of its economy. The Cao Dai, BinhXuyen and Hoa Hao had supported France against the communist insurgency in what had become South Vietnam. They were a mix of nationalist secret societies, religious cults and criminal, mafia-style, organisations, dressed up with touches of melodrama taken from a pulp novel. Paris' officials had turned a blind eye to their private armies, police forces and racketeering business. In exchange,

President Ngo Dinh Diem, the man who practically invented the Republic of Vietnam. Fiercely nationalist and anti-communist he was reasonably successful in establishing a working country. Faced with an increasingly violent communist insurgency sponsored and directed by Hanoi, his autocratic methods created dissensions between him and some of his American advisors. He was overthrown by a military coup sponsored by the US Ambassador, Henry Cabot Lodge, and some members of the State Department. (NARA)

the sects had hunted down communists. Anti-communist or not, their mere presence was a serious obstacle to any centralised state. Diem sent his infant army against them. Despite French support, the sects were defeated. This victory not only established Diem as a real player, but also forced the French to bow to his will and leave the country. The last French soldiers left South Vietnam in 1956. Diem's victory made him more popular in Washington. Collins was replaced and the United States now supported Diem, at least for the foreseeable future.

Diem's future appeared bright. US economic and technical aid allowed the restarting of the local economy, which was still suffering from the effects of Japanese occupation, Allied bombing and blockade, and nine years of war. Catholic support allowed him to fish in the largest pool of educated people in Vietnam to staff his administration. Hanoi's troubles at home, and Ho Chi Minh's typical contempt for opponents, minimised subversive interference from the North. Diem's position was also boosted by the large influx of Catholic anti-communist refugees from the North. It is worth noting that, despite repeated assertions, Diem was not a Catholic president of a Buddhist country. Catholics and Buddhists were roughly equal in numbers, but the main religion in South Vietnam was a combination of village-level ancestor cults and animistic beliefs, all mixed with Confucian, Christian and Buddhist elements. Furthermore, Catholic and Protestant missions and teachers had contributed to the creation of a large Christian, literate group that was the main reservoir for the educated people necessary to run civil and military organisations.

Diem was not without flaws, faults and detractors. He was innately suspicious and expected personal loyalty. In a country where past emperors had been, more often than not, prisoners of their own eunuchs and mandarins, this was perhaps understandable. His governing style was authoritarian and intolerant of dissent, which created increasing friction with his American friends. He was prone to use coercion rather than persuasion in political and security matters. Beside fighting the sects and rejuvenating the RVN economy, Diem launched anti-communist campaigns, with mass arrests of dissenters and torture of detained suspects. But as Mark Moyar, probably Diem's staunchest supporter among historians, points out, these traits were

The man who created the mess, Ambassador Henry Cabot Lodge. A Second World War veteran fluent in French, and former US liaison officer to General De Lattre, he was a determined anti-communist. He was also a Republican serving under a Democrat President, arrogant, and assured of American superiority. (By Eric Koch/Anefo – Nationaal Archief, CC BY-SA 3.0)

After Ambassador Lodge left Saigon to campaign with Nixon in the 1960 presidential election, retired Army General Maxwell Taylor replaced him. Outspoken and well connected, he did not work well with parts of the South Vietnamese leadership, yet he worked well with his former subordinate, MACV commander William Westmoreland, and was instrumental in the decision to commit US ground troops to Vietnam. (US Army)

also necessary to deal with a country that had been rife with dissent and gangsterism, and would have been the target of an insurgency. Arresting, torturing and killing dissenters was something that Ho Chi Minh and his cronies were also doing on a regular and large-scale basis north of the border.

Diem was also extremely confident in himself, being highly educated (in both traditional and Western institutions) and opinionated. This final trait, more than anything else, would in the end lead him to his downfall, when faced by an ally that, at times, forgot the difference between partnership and vassalage.

The other fatal flaw of Diem was that his country was virtually indefensible. Diem's Republic of Vietnam was not Rhee Syngman's Republic of Korea. Diem lacked the luxury of maritime borders that the US Navy could secure. Instead, he had a land border with Laos and Cambodia thousands of kilometres long, devoid of settlements, rich in mountain, forests and jungles. But like Rhee's Republic of Korea, there was also a powerful enemy lurking across a demilitarised zone.

Diem's Vietnamese miracle ended abruptly in late December 1959. Southern communists, supported by northern infiltrators, launched an open uprising against the RVN government. It was swift, violent and ambitious, with towns and villages in the southern part of South Vietnam, the Mekong Delta, attacked and seized. It was also short lived. The Army of the Republic of Vietnam's (ARVN) retribution was rapid and largely effective, and the initial uprising was contained and then defeated. But it was not the end. Hanoi had decided that Diem was there to stay, unless he and his government were removed by force. And force was something Hanoi was willing to use. People like Le Duan, Southern-born but now enmeshed in the Northern communist oligarchy, were determined to take Saigon by any means necessary. If a short uprising was not sufficient, a prolonged insurgency would be undertaken. If even the latter failed, there was also the People's Army of Vietnam (PAVN).

The uprising exposed fault lines with Diem's principal ally, the United States. Beside issues between Diem himself and US Ambassador Elbridge Durbrow, there was infighting between Durbrow and the principal military advisors in South Vietnam, first General Samuel Williams and then General Lionel McGarr. McGarr and Durbrow's relationship ended with both of them insulting the other in cables sent to their respective bosses in Washington. Beyond the simple personality conflict, there was an institutional rift between the State and Defense Departments about primacy in warring countries, along with a larger debate about how to deal with insurgencies and uprisings in friendly countries. This in turn was the product of a US administration that had failed to craft a sensible and well-understood security policy.

Having been elected on a platform predicated on a successful termination of the Korean War, and faced by a fractious defence establishment and a US Army staffed with officers personally hostile to him, Dwight Eisenhower's initial security policy was an unmitigated disaster.[1] His support for strategic bombardment, and thus the US Air Force, and his initial reliance on an ambiguous 'massive retaliation' policy, left the US Army unprepared to cope with conventional or unconventional conflicts. Despite a shift toward a more flexible response approach (even before President Kennedy and his Secretary of Defense Robert McNamara coined the term) during Eisenhower's second mandate, there was no real government-wide doctrine for dealing with insurgencies. While the Army had a sound approach, enshrined in Colonel Russel Volckman's *FM 31-20 Operations against Guerrilla Forces* (1951) and its subsequent iterations, there was no clear integration with civilian agencies, even if it was accepted that such operations would also be political in nature. There was no coordinating authority, and often embassies and military missions ran duplicated programmes. In Saigon, the situation was exemplified by the military mission, the Military Advisory and Assistance Group Vietnam (MAAGV), advising and supporting the ARVN, while the embassy, employing civilian universities as subcontractors, did the same with police and paramilitary groups. Furthermore, there was no real strategic direction or policy. Despite the creation of area-based 'Cold War Task Forces', there were no real guidelines for their employment, and the Task Forces themselves were still embryonic. It was no surprise that US support for Diem during 1960 was limited in nature, underfunded, tentative and inconsistent. It was not helped by infighting between US agencies, and with South Vietnamese ones. The net result was that while advisors and advisees bickered, the Viet Cong advanced. A military nuisance in January 1960, they were a problem by December that year, despite several government victories.

South Vietnam's woes were increased by a concomitant crisis in neighbouring Laos. There, a coalition government struggled with bickering between factions led by rival half-brothers, a military coup, and North Vietnamese and Soviet meddling. The situation escalated to the point that US troops had to deploy to Thailand, and SEATO (South East Asia Treaty Organisation) plans for intervention in Laos were drafted. Soviet military transports started a direct airlift from North Vietnam to Laos. Laotian troubles helped Hanoi, which had started to infiltrate troops into South Vietnam by land and sea. After the ARVN blocked direct infiltration through the DMZ, Hanoi saw Laos as a convenient corridor to bypass the DMZ and avoid the appearance of direct involvement. Of course that meant a government in Vientiane, the Laos capital, friendly to Hanoi, or at least a situation where PAVN troops could operate in Laos. In the middle of all this turmoil, in November 1960, several paratrooper battalions attempted a coup against Diem. Durbrow's support for Diem on this occasion was less than lukewarm, but loyalist troops quelled the mutiny.

Viet Cong attacks, the Laotian crisis and Durbrow's meddling prompted a reaction in Washington, where a new administration took office in January 1961. John Fitzgerald Kennedy brought with him anti-communist zeal, youth, determination and plenty of new faces. He also brought a willingness to directly confront what he saw as Soviet aggressions all across the world. This would make the United States a direct player in Vietnam for years. Yet Kennedy's first step did not appear assertive. Averell Harriman, a former US Ambassador to Stalin's Soviet Union but also a figure possessing clear anti-communist credentials, was ordered to solve the Laotian crisis. He did so by brokering a neutrality agreement that curtailed the minor US assistance to the Royal Laotian Army, but left thousands of PAVN troops there, allowing them not only to continue destabilising the country, but to set up their infiltration corridor to South Vietnam. Laotian bungling notwithstanding, the new US administration clearly committed to Diem. Durbrow was replaced by Frederick Nolting, leading to a stunning improvement in diplomatic relations. At the end of his tour in 1962, McGarr was replaced by General Paul Harkins, George Patton's Chief of Staff in the Second World War. More importantly, money, equipment and advisors were sent to South Vietnam. Diem himself also did his 'homework'. He invited a British mission, headed by Sir Robert Thompson and including Australian Army Colonel Ted Serong. Australia, South Korea and Taiwan (officially the Republic of China) also provided assistance and military advisors. The government then counterattacked; for a while, the insurgency's tide appeared to be receding.

Then another disaster struck for the South, with Frederick Nolting replaced in Saigon by Henry Cabot Lodge. A Republican presidential hopeful, Lodge was an unusual candidate for the position. He was a committed anti-communist and had served in similar roles in the past, having been the French General De Lattre de Tassigny's US Army liaison officer in 1944–45. But he was also sure of his own and American superiority over the rest of the world. His tenure in Saigon would be marred by a constant, almost dictatorial, meddling in South Vietnamese matters and a distinct ignorance of military affairs, coupled with hostility for General Harkins and an obsessive tendency to cultivate the press, largely the US press. Lodge's eyes were already set on the White House, and Saigon should have been the stepping stone. However, Lodge and Diem were soon at odds. Notwithstanding troubles at the top, on the ground there were real successes. Despite the often-touted disaster at Ap Bac – a minor action that probably more showed the incompetence of the senior US advisor on the spot, Colonel John Paul Vann, than any supposed endemic ARVN problems – the VC were being beaten consistently.[2] Yet Diem's days were numbered. Another outburst of political disturbance sealed his fate. Buddhist protests fomented by North Vietnamese agents allowed Lodge to persuade several mid-level officials in Washington to support – some would actually say foment – an Army coup in Saigon. Despite wavering from senior officials, including Kennedy himself, Lodge continued with his plotting. In November 1963, Diem was toppled and killed along with the majority of his family. Kennedy was assassinated in Dallas the same month, being succeeded by Lyndon Johnson.

Send the Marines

The November 1963 coup and Diem's subsequent death plunged the Republic of Vietnam into chaos. While the government apparatus carried on for some time, cracks were emerging. Once Diem's authoritarian but stabilising presence disappeared, everyone in a sufficiently high position of power eyed Saigon's presidential palace. Generals started bickering for power, joined by several civilian officials. Furthermore, extremist Buddhist militants and the DRV agents mixed with them demanded ever-more concessions. Each political change at the top was reflected in adjustment at the lower levels, with loyalty to power-brokers replacing loyalty to the state and competence. Military efficiency suffered accordingly, as did bureaucracy. The Anti-Catholic backlash inspired by the militant Buddhists also led to a neglect of the Catholic anti-communist militia, often the most effective local force at the government's disposal. On top of that, the US mission was savaged by an internecine conflict between Lodge and General Harkins, a staunch supporter of the deceased Diem. All the while, the NLF was increasing the numbers and quality of its military machine. Not only did the reduction in government military activity allow the VC to consolidate their control in several areas, thus increasing their recruiting pool, but more troops and equipment came south from North Vietnam too. It is little wonder that Hanoi saw Lodge's sponsored coup as a godsend.

In the midst of this bleak situation, another US Army officer came to South Vietnam, an officer whose name would be indelibly linked to the Vietnam War: General William Childs Westmoreland. Fifty years old, tall, confident and determined, Westmoreland landed in Saigon in January 1964 to fill the role of Deputy Commander, US Military Assistance Command Vietnam, the advisory group having been reorganised.[3] Westmoreland was supposed to provide "a senior experienced strong and thorough leader to get behind the advisory effort while General Harkins can devote his main attention to the politico-military sphere".[4] One of the key roles of the new arrival was to mediate between the Embassy and Military Assistance Command, Vietnam (MACV), as Harkins and Lodge refused to talk to each other. Despite what his detractors, American historian Lewis Sorley in particular, later claimed, Westmoreland brought with him considerable military experience and knowledge of counterinsurgency warfare. Graduating from West Point in 1936 as an artillery lieutenant, he served in various postings until being assigned to the 34th Artillery Battalion, 9th Infantry Division. He commanded the battalion in Tunisia and Sicily. In Tunisia, his battalion played a pivotal role in stopping the Germans after the defeat at Kasserine. Westmoreland was still with the 9th Infantry Division in 1944, but as a staff officer. In October that year, he was appointed the division Chief of Staff, and remained with the 9th until the end of the war. He then commanded the 60th Infantry Regiment in Germany, attended jump school and took charge of the 504th Parachute Infantry Regiment, part of the 82nd Airborne Division, then become the division Chief of Staff. Between 1950 and 1952, he attended the Army Command

and General Staff College as a student and then instructor. In 1952, he was promoted to brigadier general and took command of the 187th Airborne Regimental Combat Team in Japan. The regiment was acting as theatre reserve of the Eighth Army in Korea and deployed there several times. After the Korean War, he served in several staff positions in the Pentagon. In 1958, he took over the 101st Airborne Division and was involved in testing the Pentomic division concept. From 1960–62, he was West Point Military Academy superintendent. After the Korean War, Westmoreland became involved in developing, testing and disseminating COIN ideas in the US Army. As Commanding General, 101st Airborne Division, he was responsible for creating the division's first COIN course. He sponsored French Army officer and COIN theorist David Galula when he applied for a doctorate in the US. As West Point Superintendent, he also successfully pressed for COIN courses there. The same interest marked his tenure as XVIII Airborne Corps commander in 1962–63.

General William C. Westmoreland, the man who came to define the American involvement in Vietnam in the 1965-1968 period. A career artillery officer and graduate of West Point in, and a veteran of both the Second World War and Korea, he was an early supporter of the development of US Counterinsurgency Doctrine. Once at the helm of MACV he had to chart a difficult course between Vietnamese political instability, pacification of the countryside, a growing number of enemy divisions, and his political bosses in Washington. (US Army)

The US Army had never abandoned COIN during Eisenhower's years in office. While authors like Cable, Krepinevich and Doughty have depicted a US Army paying only lip services to an administration infatuated with counterinsurgency, the reality was different. The US Army led COIN development even before Kennedy and his main COIN advisor, Walt Rostow, made it the staple of US military assistance through the Overseas Internal Defense Policy (OIDP). The OIDP assumed that insurgencies were primarily political struggles to redress social and economic grievances, and thus prescribed a series of vigorous measures ranging from political and economic reforms to military actions. While it is true that the US Army was a global force with global missions, it invested resources in developing and testing an effective COIN doctrine in the OIDP's framework. In 1963, a White House report affirmed that the Army, and to a lesser extent the Marines, were the only organisations that had seriously embraced their roles in the OIDP. Not only did the US Army possess a sound doctrine as enunciated in its new FM 15-31 Field Manual by 1963, but it had put this doctrine to the test through several exercises up to division-size. The 25th Infantry Division in Hawaii, the Pacific Command contingency reserve, was running guerrilla training course and had even created training villages. Westmoreland had not only supported Galula's immigration to the United States, but also used him and the more controversial Colonel Paul Aussares to give lectures at West Point.

Marines from the 9th Expeditionary Brigade (soon to be renamed 9th Amphibious Brigade) land at Da Nang in March 1965. While not the first US soldiers in Vietnam, several tens of thousands were already in the country, they were the first combat units deployed. (USMC)

While COIN had become a cornerstone of US policy through the OIDP, the various departments and agencies were still wrangling with problems of command, subordination and cooperation, the two big and apparently irreconcilable players being the State and Defense Departments. At the political level, calling the shots was more important than winning on the ground. High-level wrangling was not the only issue. Exercises had hinted at problems with the military aspect of COIN itself. Brigade and division commanders highlighted limits of the effectiveness of civic action in changing people's thinking.[5] Furthermore, economic aid, civic action and all the economic measures designed to stop the 'spread of the communist virus' depended on military security, but the whole COIN concept

Following the Marines, the 173rd Airborne Brigade deployed from Okinawa to Vietnam. Here troopers from the brigade unload from a USAF C-130 at Vung Tau airfield on 5 May 1965. Note the brigade had already been equipped with M16 rifles. (US Army)

While initially deployed to protect US airbases, US troops soon engaged in direct combat operations. As USMC General Lewis Walt argued, no one had won a war sitting on his ration box. The Marines were the first to engage, with the now expanded III Marine Amphibious Force launching Operation STARLITE in August 1965 against the 1st NLF Regiment in the north part of South Vietnam. Here Marines from D Company 1-7th Marines are on the lookout for snipers during the battle. (USMC)

the US Army was not just wedded to conventional war, its COIN doctrine was wedded to social, political and military understandings that were far from perfect.

Nevertheless, when William Westmoreland arrived in Saigon, he was one of the most qualified US Army general officers in COIN matters. He also believed in COIN. His priority as MACV Deputy Commander was clearly to rejuvenate pacification. He also worked hard to restore, if not confidence, then at least a workable relationship between the MACV and the Embassy. His efforts were marked by mixed results. Certainly his burden eased when both Harkins (in May 1964) and Lodge (in June of the same year) left Saigon, Lodge to plunge into the 1964 presidential campaign. Westmoreland took over as COMUSMACV (Commander, US Military Assistance Command, Vietnam), while his old Army patron, General Maxwell Taylor, replaced Lodge. The team was now at least functioning properly. Westmoreland was also able to build an effective relationship with the new ARVN Chief of Staff, General Cao Van Vien. Through a combination of personal friendship and subtle persuasion, relations with the ARVN high command were improved. From a high command standpoint, Westmoreland did indeed produce a marked improvement.

In the field, the situation was different. Emphasising that doctrine was one thing and reality another, the whole OIDP framework was already

was predicated on facing poorly armed guerrillas. In this regard, the 'popularity' of COIN with the new administration had created a deleterious effect, with the doctrine anchored to academic political science with its inflexible models rather than military strategy. Kennedy and his principal advisor, Rostow, did not really consider the possibility of an opponent embracing direct conventional or semi-conventional tactics. The deputy US Army Chief of Staff, General Lyman Lenmitzer, had presciently highlighted the problems of facing a more heavily equipped enemy. But Lenmitzer's caveats were left unaddressed in the OIDP, based on the assumption that insurgencies would have been quashed before reaching such a stage. Thus, while

collapsing. The ARVN was not yet fully recommitted to the struggle, with coups and counter-coups continuing until mid-1965, and by the end of 1964 it was hopelessly outgunned. Hanoi and NLF leaders had decided to counter Diem's COIN counteroffensive of 1962–63 with an escalation of their own. Not only did the PAVN provide better weapons to local insurgents, but it started sending battalions, then regiments, then divisions south. By December 1964, the communists were engaging in multi-regiment clashes, such as the Battle of Binh Gia. Westmoreland found himself facing a dilemma. COIN doctrine and common sense required government forces to spread out to provide security in the rural areas, but doing that only invited NLF regiments to pounce on ARVN companies and platoons. Losing battles demoralised the ARVN and forced it to relinquish the initiative in the countryside. Furthermore, without the ARVN, government presence was non-existent.

The ARVN itself was part of the problem. Leaving aside the debate on its motivation, morale and leadership, it was not equipped for serious fighting. It was an army built on the cheap on the premise that if serious fighting erupted, it would have been a conventional invasion, whereupon either US or SEATO forces would have come to the rescue; or, when Eisenhower was in office, Hanoi and Beijing would have been nuked in a show of massive retaliation, impractical as that may have been. Even after January 1961, the Kennedy administration had not changed the whole structure. The MACV had introduced small quantities of newer equipment, but the ARVN was still largely equipped with surplus Second World War-vintage equipment. In the worst cases, especially regarding vehicles, they had been previously used by US troops in the Second World War and then by the French in the 1945–54 struggle in Indochina, making them third-hand equipment. Even if the official COIN doctrine stressed the importance of infantry automatic firepower, what the ARVN had at platoon level were just M1 Garands, M1 Carbines and BARs to counter not just SKS carbines, but also significant numbers of AK-47s and their Chinese copies. It is worth noting that the 'massive retaliation' policy had impacted the US Army to the point that its standard equipment was not much better. The M16 assault rifle was a limited issue item in 1964, and the M60 light machine gun was only just entering service. Even increased aid after January 1961 had not changed the ARVN, largely because the US could supply only what it had available.

Apart from the ARVN, there was nothing else to protect the South Vietnam government's authority. Diem's paramilitary organisations, built after prolonged infighting between the MAAGV and the Embassy, had been gutted for political reasons. They remained effective only in Catholic areas, but relying on these caused friction with the extreme element of the Buddhist movement. The few areas where those militias were still effective also became primary targets for NLF attacks. Binh Gia had one of the last self-defence organisations, and was the scene of the first division-size battle of the Vietnam War. In that situation, COIN did no good for Westmoreland. He was forced to admit that the ARVN was losing the equivalent of a battalion per week, with no appreciable results to show in return. Later, in his writings, he compared the fighting in Vietnam to protecting a house threatened by termites (the guerrilla forces) and bullies with crowbars (the enemy's conventional forces). While the termites would have eventually destroyed the house, the bullies were tearing it apart right now. Thus, nothing short of a decisive change of strategy could have stemmed the tide in Vietnam.

Stemming the Tide

This foreboding attitude was not just pervading MACV but was shared by Ambassador Taylor and the whole Johnson administration in Washington. The consensus was that, barring some form of direct American commitment, South Vietnam would be lost. Debates centred on the kind of commitment necessary and its worth to the global position of the United States. In a period dominated by the so-called domino theory – and with communist insurgencies going on in several countries across the globe, Soviet influence in the Middle East on the rise and a feeling that Washington needed to assert its commitment to containment – conflict was inevitable. Communist insurgencies in South Korea, Laos and Malaysian Borneo made the question of commitment even more pressing. There was thus a broad consensus on the necessity for action, but what such action should entail to save South Vietnam was much less clear.

While the Marines were expanding their area of operations around Da Nang, US Army units, chiefly the 173rd Airborne Brigade, were doing the same in the area around Saigon. Here troopers from the 173rd are preparing for an heliborne operation, 27 May 1965. (US Army)

Troopers of the 173rd Brigade boarding helicopters in the same operation. (US Army)

Elements of the 173rd Airborne Brigade, after having disembarked from the UH-1Bs, deploy to secure their landing zone's perimeter, 19 May 1965. (US Army)

Dismounted element of the 16th Armor Battalion, usually equipped with M56 Scorpion tank destroyers, patrol the jungle in a hitherto unexplored area controlled by the Viet Cong. 28 September 1965. (US Army)

The US Air Force, US Navy and the USMC recommended a massive strike on North Vietnam to persuade Hanoi to halt its aggression. This course of action was also recommended by Walt Rostow. However, the US Army favoured a ground campaign to stem the tide in South Vietnam, something that also appealed to McNamara, the Secretary of Defense. President Johnson, more worried by the November 1964 elections, demurred and tried to proceed by small, almost tentative, steps to keep as much control as possible at the top, something favoured also by McNamara. A small series of air attacks, Operation PIERCE ARROW, was launched in August 1964 as an immediate response to two attacks (one real, one still muddled in the fog of war and primitive radar plots) on the USS *Maddox*, a US Navy destroyer. By spring 1965, Johnson's advisors coalesced around a limited, gradual air campaign coupled with deployment of combat troops to South Vietnam. As was usually the case, major commitments were taken without a clear endgame strategy.

In practice, a Marine Expeditionary Brigade was first sent ashore at Da Nang to protect the airfield and the air and air defence units based there for strikes on North Vietnam. Then the 173rd Airborne Brigade was sent Bien Hoa, north-east of Saigon, to protect USAF aircraft based there. More US troops then followed. Yet neither troop deployments nor airstrikes on North Vietnam changed the situation. At best they were ignored; at worst they prompted an acceleration of the military campaign to finish South Vietnam before more US troops could deploy. The North Vietnamese missions also changed. In March 1965, a Vietnamese Special Forces camp at Dong Xoai was attacked by a full enemy regiment. Other enemy units deployed to ambush relief forces, as they had done at Binh Gia in December, and the first ARVN reaction force was mauled. Increased USAF close air support (CAS) was requested by Westmoreland, as was permission to deploy the 173rd in support of the camp. Permission was granted, but, in the end, the commitment was not required, CAS turning the tide at the 11th hour. Further clarification was sought from MACV about the ability to use US troops for similar missions in the future. Almost as an afterthought, Johnson and McNamara granted it. From then onward, Washington and Hanoi were on a collision course.

Back in Hanoi, Vo Nguyen Giap, Ho Chi Minh's confidant, Minister of Defense and Commander in Chief, sensed the collapse of the ARVN and brushed aside doubts about an intensified military campaign. He said his troops would have won in the field before American troops were deployed in sufficient numbers. Not only would the tide have turned, but the Americans would have been humiliated. Westmoreland, however, was determined to stem the tide. He attacked first near the Phuoc Thuan peninsula, between Da Nang and Hue. In Operation STARLITE, a reinforced USMC regiment surprised the 1st VC Regiment and smashed it. Giap responded with a division-sized attack in the Central Highlands toward Pleiku conducted by a PAVN division. Westmoreland replied by deploying his latest reinforcement, the 1st Cavalry Division (Airmobile), to support the ARVN troops in the area under Operation SILVER BAYONET. The two formations clashed in November in the Ia Drang Valley, with both sides subsequently claiming victory. At the same time, the 173rd Airborne engaged enemy forces in the Saigon area. The tide was to be stemmed after all.

Attrition

The introduction of American combat forces in Vietnam in the spring of 1965, and their intervention in the fighting in the summer and autumn of the same year, did not alter Hanoi's strategy or tactics. For the planners in Hanoi and the commanders of the various Fronts managing operations in the territory of the Republic of Vietnam, large units and high-intensity war was still the answer to all their troubles. The goal was attrition. There is no evidence that in 1965 Hanoi planned a shift in tactics or a return to guerrilla warfare. It was believed that main force units would be the key to victory against the Americans

The other side of US Army operation in Vietnam, civic action. In this picture taken on 28 September 1965, troopers distribute food, clothing, and candies for children in front of Ben Cat district HQ. (US Army)

The enemy, here regular People Army of Vietnam troops. Well-trained and well-equipped, they often outgunned South Vietnamese troops at this stage of war and were a dangerous opponent also for US troops, as the battle of Dau Tieng would reveal. (Albert Grandolini)

as they had been against the French. The bottom line was that Giap saw the Americans in the same light he had the French two decades earlier. Not just that, but documents have made clear that he was expecting to win his main force war before US troops could make their presence felt. This was even after Operations STARLITE and SILVER BAYONET. It is important to note that he committed to his Pleiku campaign after STARLITE and was still expecting to face only ARVN troops. This should at least cast some doubt on the claims about his military genius.

Of course, continuing with the then current strategy had advantages. After the collapse of Diem's government, the ARVN was the glue keeping South Vietnam together. It was not a mystery, and was noted by DRV, GVN and US observers. Destroying the ARVN would have doomed anyone sitting in the Presidential Palace in Saigon. That was what happened in 1975. Hitting the ARVN hard was a logical and worthwhile military target. The counterpoint to that is that, after August 1965, hitting the ARVN would have also involved US troops in one way or another. Yet from a military standpoint, the leadership of the PAVN and PLAF was confident that US troops would not have posed any special problem. If there was some apprehension before the first encounter, the glowing reports filtering upward in November 1965 put these to rest. Issues with PAVN and PLAF battlefield 'successes' will be further discussed in Chapter 4, but for now it is necessary to mention that almost every engagement between PAVN or PLAF forces and American units was reported as a success. More often than not, US forces involved were exaggerated in number.

According to communist officers, American battalions were routinely destroyed. A typical case was Operation STARLITE, known to the communists as the Battle of Van Tuong. Communist reports described it as an American 'Stalingrad',[6] with claims that they defeated an operation conducted by eight Marine battalions.[7] According to the same self-aggrandising reports, 919 Marines were killed, with 22 US vehicles and 13 helicopters destroyed. Interestingly, only one rifle was captured in the course of this stunning victory. The truth was somewhat different. Only thee Marine battalions participated in the operation. Furthermore, STARLITE had cost the 1st VC Regiment more than 600 KIA (killed in action) and scores of wounded, the 'eight' Marine battalions suffering only 45 KIA and 203 wounded. The 1st VC Regiment had faced USMC combined arms teams and had been mauled. Yet the regiment fed a different story up its chain

The other enemy, local NLF guerrillas. Badly equipped, with variable motivation, they were nevertheless an important factor in the struggle for control of South Vietnam. Here a group of young NLF guerrilla appears to be undergoing some political indoctrination session. There was no standard equipment, and uniforms could vary from khaki fatigues to normal civilian clothes, yet note the two AK-47s carried. (Albert Grandolini)

of command. Later, some officers started to recognise a "decoupling of battlefield reporting and battlefield reality", but this would only happen after 1967.[8] In 1968, a perceptive officer stated:

> We can see that reporting from subordinate commanders to their superiors did not accurately reflect the real situation. Successes were usually exaggerated and mistakes and failures were not reported. This had a significant impact on our operations. It causes senior commanders to misjudge and misevaluate the situation, which in turn led them to make incorrect policy decisions and to set goals and objectives which were unattainable.[9]

The 'victories' of the autumn of 1965 helped in the crafting of a strategy of attrition on Hanoi's side. Buoyed by the purported destruction of entire American battalions, Giap and his subordinates assumed they would be capable of bleeding the US Army and the USMC white before suffering crippling losses. In the meantime, they also planned to continue their onslaught against the ARVN. For Hanoi, the 'American War' would have been a main force war based on attrition. The Americans were considered a weak adversary. A report dated 3 July 1965 maintained the US troops were poor opponents: "No spirit of combat; afraid of guerrillas, always rely on modern weapons, so they lose initiative and self-confidence (when in contact, they call for fire support and reinforcement); sometimes artillery must conduct fire support for the whole period of the operation."[10]

North Vietnamese officers derided American tactics and supporting arms, taunting their opponents as being cowards.[11] Of course, part of these criticisms were a product of a carefully worded comparison of 'popular' and 'imperialist' fighting styles, but it is undeniable that plenty of reports, writings and even post-war personal memoirs show a misplaced sense of superiority in themselves and their tactical methods. The bottom line was the North Vietnamese military leadership underestimated their opponents, something that they had also often done with the French. Underestimation coupled with unreliable battlefield reporting assured the communist leadership that their own main force units were winning, inflicting disproportionate casualties on their opponent. Armed with such evidence, the Twelfth Plenum of the Vietnamese Communist Party decided not only to continue the struggle and prepare for the eventuality of a prolonged war, but to escalate military commitment in the South to achieve a decisive victory.[12]

Not that this conclusion was unanimous, as Hanoi – like Washington – experienced debates between various factions and currents. There was a sizeable minority that advocated retrenchment and even negotiation. This minority not only comprised 'North-First' politicians, but also NLF leaders from the South, arguing that military methods were not bringing victory. Yet an alliance of military men, hardliners and Southern-born communists living in Hanoi was persuaded that a decisive military blow could be struck in 1966. They assumed that their troops could kill approximately 60,000 Americans and 20,000 South Vietnamese in a year, a target that would even be revised upward by subordinate commands. For example, COSVN (the Central Office for South Vietnam, the North's political and military headquarters south of the border) set as its military target the killing of 30,000–40,000 US troops and 200,000 of the ARVN, and the destruction of 1,000 aircraft, for 1966 alone.[13] They were also persuaded that only the so-called 'Big Unit' war could meet these quotas. At this point it is important to highlight that what General William DePuy of the US 1st Division called the 'Reinforced Main Force War' was not an American construct, but something Hanoi instigated and waged with relish. Battalion and even regiment/brigade-size battles were not anomalies in an otherwise guerrilla war; they were the norm rather than the exception. Giap's strategy was a 'Regular Force Strategy',[14] which aimed for a quick, decisive military victory.[15] To back words with deeds, Hanoi sent nine more infantry regiments and three artillery regiments south in 1966, which would be a year of very big battles indeed.

The American Response

Tactically stemming the enemy offensive was not enough for the US. To be successful in preserving South Vietnam as a non-communist state, the tide had to be turned. Westmoreland's mission was more complex than simply stopping the 1965 offensive. From a strategic viewpoint, at least for the White House, MACV's mission was persuading the enemy, Hanoi, that victory in the South was impossible. Of course, such an ill-defined goal required clearer orders. Sadly, these orders were never directly issued from Washington, where the President and the Secretary of Defense seemed content to leave MACV judging how to achieve their goals while they managed other elements of the war. From Westmoreland's perspective, even ill-defined broad goals involved more than just reacting to enemy initiative. To prevent

Beside fighting the communist insurgency, both South Vietnamese and US troops had often to deal with political riots in the major cities of Saigon, Hue, and Da Nang. This picture depicts South Vietnamese soldiers clearing demonstrators in Saigon in 1966. (US Army)

an enemy takeover of South Vietnam and fulfil his mission, the MACV's commander had to tackle several issues almost simultaneously: he had to stabilise the government in Saigon, reverse NLF territorial gain in the countryside and militarily defeat the PAVN and PLAF main force units.

The latter element was extremely important. As already discussed in his own writings, General Westmoreland equated the main forces to bullies armed with crowbars, the guerrillas to termites and South Vietnam to a wooden house. Both groups would have torn it down, but the bullies would have done it faster. Losing district or, even worse, provincial capitals would have doomed Saigon's government. Destroying ARVN battalions, meanwhile, would have left the government bereft of reliable forces to oppose the guerrillas. As General DePuy said after the war, by 1964, beside the insurgency there was also a main force war going on.[16] Ignoring this would have just repeated the Binh Dinh disaster on a larger scale. Furthermore, Hanoi was too enmeshed in the conflict for a simple show of force to be effective. As Westmoreland cautioned the Chief of the Joint Chiefs of Staff, General Earle Wheeler, they were "too deeply committed to be influenced by anything but application of overpowering force".[17] To provide anything useful to Johnson, Westmoreland had to reverse the military situation in South Vietnam.

The methods employed by Westmoreland to defeat the communists in South Vietnam has always been the focus of acrimonious debate, especially after 1975. For some, William Childs Westmoreland was 'the general who lost Vietnam'. For others, he was a competent officer faced with a gargantuan task and limited resources. There is more truth in the latter contention than the former. Accusing Westmoreland and his officers at MACV of having tried to create a different war just to appease a supposed US Army penchant for conventional conflict is disingenuous at best.[18] As Dale Andrade noted, MACV had to fight two wars at the same time. Going after the main force units was not a luxury but a necessity. There was no doubt that the insurgency could have been defeated only in populated areas, but these areas had to be provided security first. They had to be protected by marauding regiments and divisions. This was the basic tenet of Westmoreland's decisions and strategy. He needed to literally kick the main forces out with American troops.

Westmoreland was clearly aware of the issues and tried to craft a strategy that was both balanced and flexible enough to deal with the dual threat. At its core, it was simple: "Without military security, none of the other political, social and economic programs sponsored by Saigon and Washington would have made much headway."[19] On top of that, in 1965 the ARVN was not capable of assuring military security. Its divisions, regiments and battalions had suffered too much. US troops would have to provide a shield behind which the ARVN could recover and, steadily, return to the countryside. As Karl von Clausewitz said, everything is simple, but in war simple things become complex. MACV's problems stemmed from logistical and operational considerations. The US Army was neither large enough nor had sufficient logistical infrastructure in South Vietnam to instantly conjure a massive expeditionary force in theatre from nothing. US combat troops would only trickle into Vietnam according to manpower availability and the improvements to the logistical infrastructure. In turn this meant that any significant operation and operational concept would require time to implement.

Thus, Westmoreland had to work in phases. Phase I, concomitant with the introduction of the first significant ground combat elements in Vietnam, would see US troops creating the logistical infrastructure, building bases to protect critical cities, and when necessary launching spoiling attacks against enemy concentrations. Operation SILVER BAYONET and the following actions in the Ia Drang Valley stemmed from these spoiling attacks. They protected Pleiku and the Central Highlands and gave time for Westmoreland to introduce more troops. At the same time, as will be discussed in more detail in Chapter 4, the 1st Infantry Division tried to keep PLAF forces around Saigon off balance, buying time for more American troops to deploy in the region.

Once enough troops were deployed, Westmoreland could switch to his own Phase II, a general offensive. US and allied troops, with the support of a rejuvenated ARVN, would launch a drive into enemy sanctuaries to engage and destroy PAVN and PLAF main force units. This sustained offensive phase would drive major enemy units away from populated areas and remove the main armed backers of the local guerrillas from the equation. The aim was to create "an environment within which the larger pacification program could proceed".[20] Hopefully, at that point Hanoi would have been decisively defeated and willing to concede. If not, a Phase III would be implemented. This would have seen the shift of US resources from large-scale battles, now assumed to have been won, to direct support of pacification programs. If Phase II was built around the necessity to eradicate

Riots could also turn violent. (US Army)

Focusing on just the local guerrillas and ignoring enemy main force units, as has been advocated by countless COIN-ista writers, was simply impossible. The COIN critique of MACV had always been predicated on the idea that in 1965, MACV had a choice: either going conventional or going COIN. But the choice was never there. Probably the most significant endorsement of the MACV decision came from the Australian Army, an army that had built a considerable reputation for understanding insurgencies. According to historian Dale Andrade, Westmoreland simply did not have a choice.[22] It was Hanoi which had added the conventional dimension to the war in 1964, if not in 1963. MACV had to fight the enemy main force units and keep them away. The usual contention that only replicating the British strategy in Malaya would have led to success in Vietnam was baseless. While British COIN expert Sir Robert Thompson stated that "myself and my colleagues on the British Advisory Mission to Vietnam, all remarked that we found nothing new [compared to Malaya] except in scale and intensity", Australian Lieutenant General John Coates remarked that "one of the most observed statements made by Australian Army officers who fought in both campaigns, was that difference in scale and intensity between the two conflicts made all the difference in the world".[23] There was no alternative to Westmoreland's approach. Even the much-lauded Provisional Report on Vietnam (PROVN), often cited as a severe criticism of Westmoreland's approach, reached this conclusion.[24] According to the report, a prerequisite for pacification was, "The deployment of US and FWMAF (Free World Military Assistance Forces) to destroy PAVN and Main Force VC units and base areas and to reduce external support."[25] MACV did not have alternatives.

enemy conventional forces from South Vietnam, Phase III was predicated upon keeping them away. It is important to highlight that in the MACV campaign plan, while the emphasis on the role of US troops was to fight enemy large units, in the whole plan this element was just a means to an end. Furthermore, while there was a division of labour between US and other allied troops – such as the ANZAC and Republic of Korea contingents – on one side and the ARVN on the other, it was a flexible division. US and other allied troops would participate directly in pacification and the ARVN in offensive operations when productive.

Looking at this plan, it is difficult to find any reason to label the approach as controversial.[21] It is also worth noting that the two alternatives usually proposed – General Maxwell Taylor's enclave strategy and its variations, or Andrew Krepinevich's counterinsurgency focus – were largely impracticable. Taylor's idea, to use US troops to secure enclaves in the populated coastal lowlands while the ARVN battled enemy regular forces, clearly appears the weakest alternative. There were three issues that Westmoreland pointed out at the time. First, such a strategy would have ceded large areas of South Vietnam to the enemy, weakening the prestige of the government, but also virtually handing the initiative to the enemy. It also relegated US forces, with all their firepower, mobility, combat training and massive resources, to a static mission contrary to their doctrine, either conventional or COIN. Finally, there was a major problem with the idea of sending the ARVN to fight enemy main forces. As has been discussed, the primary reason for deploying large American combat units to Vietnam was the near collapse of the ARVN. Sending depleted, under-equipped and poorly supported ARVN battalions to be trounced by communist main force units appeared in direct contradiction to the commitment of US troops. If someone should have gone into the jungle and the highlands to square off against PAVN and PLAF forces, it should have been fresh and well-trained American troops that were backed by plenty of firepower.

One of the most overused military axioms is that in war, no plan survives contact with the enemy. Westmoreland's plan not only had to survive contact with a flexible and apparently competent enemy, but also with an overall logistical and personnel situation created by local conditions and decisions in Washington. Initially, MACV hoped to end its Phase I by December 1965 and shift in full gear to Phase II in January 1966. By the start of Phase II, MACV counted on having around 20 combat brigade equivalents of US and other allied troops available for offensive operations. The timetable was important, because the months between October and March afforded the best weather for military operation in the majority of South Vietnam. The end of March heralded the arrival of the wet monsoon season and its worsening weather conditions. Wet monsoons brought with them rain and fog. Not only did ground conditions deteriorate, but the weather was not conducive to airmobile operations. Considering that helicopters were assumed to be a mainstay of US mobility, weather was an important consideration. Once Phase II started, MACV hoped to continue a maximum offensive effort for the whole of 1966 and the first few months of 1967. By April 1967, Westmoreland hoped the enemy main force would have been sufficiently smashed to remove them from the equation.[26]

The reality was rather different. After an initial surge of troops in 1965, President Johnson's decision to not mobilise reserves, logistical bottlenecks and the multiple commitments of the US military slowed down deployments to Vietnam. As an example, the 25th Infantry Division, Pacific Command's reserve that had trained specifically for Vietnam for several years, did not deploy to Vietnam, despite Westmoreland's requests, until late December 1965. Troop deployment picked up pace after the summer of 1965, but not in the strength MACV had requested. While full divisions were committed in August (1st Cavalry Division) and September (1st Infantry Division), their deployment took time. At the end of 1965, while the total personnel in Vietnam had climbed from 24,000 to 185,000, MACV could field only the equivalent of 13 brigades, compared to the 15 that Westmoreland considered necessary for his Phase I. Worse still, only by October 1966 would the logistical infrastructure needed to support the required combat forces be in place. While MACV had forces to conduct spoiling attacks, it had not the resources required to switch to an overall offensive posture. This allowed Hanoi to continue its own build-up in South Vietnam, forcing MACV to increase its force requirements for offensive operations. Both sides were simultaneously building their forces. Early 1966 saw the arrival of the rest of the 25th Infantry Division, but there was then a pause between February and July. Only in late July did the troops' deployment resume in strength. From then until January 1967, MACV would receive two infantry divisions (the 4th and 9th), two separate infantry brigades (the 196th and 199th) and one armored cavalry regiment (the 11th). Individual battalions would be deployed to fill vacant slots in deployed formations, but, even more importantly, there would be an increase in the amount of corps troops, especially aviation and artillery. In January 1967, MACV also expected to field a special riverine force around a brigade of the 9th Infantry Division for offensive operation in the Mekong Delta region. The Korean 9th Infantry Division would also deploy to Vietnam in 1966, joining the Capital Division and the 2nd Marine Brigade already there from 1965. Australian and New Zealand forces would also expand their presence in 1966, from a battalion to a full brigade-size task force. In the northern provinces of South Vietnam, 1966 would see the arrival of the 1st Marine Division and the 26th Marine Regiment to support the 3rd Marine Division already there. Completing the build-up, more and more USAF squadrons would deploy in Vietnam or Thailand to support ground operations and increase air operation against North Vietnam.

A delayed MACV Phase II offensive would have started in January 1967, first in the southern and central region of the country, exploiting the dry season; then, with the wet season coming and the concomitant improvement in weather conditions in the northern section of the country, MACV would have shifted its attention northward. For MACV, 1967 was supposed to be the year of the offensive. MACV was in a race with Hanoi. Both sides wanted to land their knockout blow on their opponent. Hanoi hoped to land it in 1966, but MACV had resigned itself to doing it in 1967 while spoiling the enemy in the meantime. It was still to be seen whether Westmoreland's build-up and spoiling attacks would prove to be enough.

2

THE COMMUNISTS: THE PEOPLE'S ARMY OF VIETNAM AND THE PEOPLE'S LIBERATION ARMED FORCES

One of the most enduring images of the Vietnam War are black-clad local guerrillas courageously opposing a bumbling army of badly trained, poorly motivated conscripts from the United States relying only on overwhelming artillery and air support to survive. This has been constantly rehashed by several Vietnamese and American writers for their own reasons, but it did not reflect any reality on the ground. This enduring image is both wrong and misleading. By the end of the summer of 1965, the war had evolved into a confrontation between conventional armies. Each of these armies had its strengths, weaknesses and defining characteristics. As already discussed, while the 'insurgency' that had characterised the 1959–63 period had not disappeared, from 1964 onward, Hanoi had steadily shifted toward a big unit war designed to knock down its opponent in a series of catastrophic blows. To carry this policy, the main instrument of war was the regular divisions and regiments of both the People's Army of North Vietnam (PAVN) and its southern clone, the People's Liberation Armed Forces (PLAF). While the primary target of these formations was the Army of the Republic of Vietnam (ARVN), the state of near collapse of the ARVN had forced Washington to put its own regular units in the frontline. This meant that while ARVN units and other South Vietnamese forces would operate around Saigon, the focus of Operation ATTLEBORO would be the fight by the US Army units deployed around Saigon.

Considered by some one of the greatest military geniuses of the 20th century, and by others just a mediocre commander who used his political connections to hide his failures, Vo Nguyen Giap (1911-2013) combined the positions of Minister of Defense and Commander of the People's Army of Vietnam. His role in supporting the big unit war his subordinates were waging in the South is controversial. (Public domain)

One of the most confusing aspects of Hanoi's war in South Vietnam was the existence of two largely parallel military organisations: the PAVN and the PLAF. The former was clearly a 'foreign' expeditionary force sent south to wage a large-scale war, while the latter was ostensibly the outgrowth of the 'indigenous' NLF. By 1966, both were largely comprised of North Vietnamese recruits and staffed by North Vietnamese officers, while some PLAF units were even organised in North Vietnam, but the distinction remained for propaganda purposes. Furthermore, considering PLAF units have always been reported in US documents as VC units, some commentators used this difference to portray them as guerrilla rather than regular infantry formations, thus reinforcing the myth of the 'foolishness' of Westmoreland's 'big unit' war. Organisationally speaking, the differences were spurious; some PAVN divisions even included PLAF regiments and vice versa. These divisions were used as they were part of the same army, the nomenclature becoming more and more just an honorific. This also meant that both shared the same common traits.

Well equipped and well-armed, People's Liberation Armed Forces, the so-called main force units, were a far cry from the guerrillas of 1960. They fought in regular formations up to division level. Here an unidentified unit from the B-2 Front is parading for the camera. Note the AK-47 being standard equipment, and the recoilless rifles, Soviet heavy machine guns (on the right), and an array of light and heavy mortars. PLAF and PAVN infantry unit incorporated a much greater quantity of heavy weapons than their US counterparts. (Albert Grandolini)

Regarding common traits, the first one is the supposed historical competence of the PAVN. It is common to see the PAVN that fought the Americans in 1966 described as the same one that defeated the French at Dien Bien Phu. This approach simply ignores dates and procedures. Like its American counterpart, the PAVN and PLAF was a large, conscripted army. It was also an army that had enlarged considerably between 1954 and 1966. From 1963 onward, it was engaged in a constantly expanding war in South Vietnam. That meant that while senior officers had combat experience, the rank and file fighters were younger. Battalion and company commanders had often reached their position due to party connections or education. Training in Soviet or Chinese military schools was as important as battlefield experience, as in any army. Furthermore, combat attrition, especially for the PLAF, had ensured that while combat-experienced cadres were available, new, often badly or partly trained recruits filled the ranks. By the same token, even if often neglected by writers, the US Army and USMC had their share of combat veterans with two wars under their belts – the Second World War and Korea – yet the army was not the same one which had defeated the Third Reich, Imperial Japan and both the Korean People's Army and the Chinese People's Liberation Army.

One of the reasons for the abundance of heavy weapons at lower levels was the poor state of communications. Radios were in short supply and due to the need for power often confined to battalion or regimental HQs if not higher ones. In this image a hand-cranked generator is used to power a radio set. (Albert Grandolini)

The 9th People's Liberation Armed Forces Division

All North Vietnamese units operating in the broadly defined Saigon region fell under the control of the B-2 Front. For ATTLEBORO, the B-2 Front's 9th PLAF Division was the main communist formation. While units from other commands and formations were engaged, almost all came under the tactical command of the 9th PLAF Division during this period. The 9th Division itself had the distinction of being the first regular division formed by the National Liberation Front in South Vietnam. It was officially organised on 3 September 1965 and had its first engagements in November of the same year. The division comprised three infantry regiments: the 271st, 272nd and 273rd. In some Vietnamese sources, the three regiments are simply listed as the 1st, 2nd and 3rd Regiments of the 9th Division, yet in the majority of accounts of the October and November 1966 battles they are identified with their previously stated numbering and this convention will be followed here. Supporting the three infantry regiments, the division possessed artillery, mortar, anti-aircraft, reconnaissance and engineering units oscillating between battalion and company size. PLAF and PAVN units tended to follow triangular organisational patterns, with supporting arms at regimental and divisional level. For example, the 273rd Regiment comprised three infantry battalions, one artillery/heavy weapons battalion, one mortar company and the usual reconnaissance, anti-aircraft, engineers, transportation and medical

The common image of the Viet Cong, a popular militia equipped of a hodgepodge of weapons. Here local forces stage a firepower demonstration for the photographer with old US-made M1 and M2 carbines. (Albert Grandolini)

The reality was much different, a young communist soldier equipped with a Chinese-manufactured AK-47 (Type 56) with fixed bayonet, and the typical three-pouch ammo rig. (Albert Grandolini)

units in company-strength. An infantry battalion was composed of three infantry companies and one heavy weapons company.

While the PLAF's organisation was neat and professional on paper, this was only a theoretical organisation. Losses, transfers and assorted campaign vagaries combined to make units in the field, especially during prolonged campaigns, less standardised. This was especially true for the artillery battalions. During ATTLEBORO, the 9th Division did not field any conventional tube artillery. Indirect fire support was the preserve of mortar battalions and companies. The artillery battalions often fielded combinations of recoilless rifles, heavy machine guns and the ubiquitous mortars. Even recoilless rifles were an assortment of US-made types (57mm, 75mm and 106mm), along with Soviet versions or Chinese copies of the latter. This hodgepodge of heavy weapons created logistical nightmares and contributed to their relative rarity on the battlefield.

On the other hand, by 1966, standard infantry weapons appear to have been plentiful and standardised. Far from the image of a pyjama-clad, sandal-wearing militiaman carrying an obsolete rifle, the typical PLAF infantryman was a well equipped and usually well trained soldier sporting top-of-the-line equipment for the period. Soviet and Chinese largesse, coupled with a well-established supply network not yet dented by American air and naval interdiction, had made possible the equipping of both the PAVN and PLAF main units with weapons equal or even superior to those of their adversaries. By 1966, their standard infantry weapon was the Soviet AK-47 assault rifle, or its Chinese copy. Less common was the Soviet SKS carbine, which was still an effective and reasonably modern weapon. At platoon level, Soviet Degtayrev 7.62mm light machine guns provided sustained fire. Again at platoon level in PLAF units and sometimes at squad level in PAVN ones, there were Soviet RPGs: either the RPG-2 or the newer RPG-7. According to communist sources, the latter weapons system gave Viet Cong and PAVN soldiers a decisive firepower advantage over their opponents. One NVA officer said:

> The American infantry units are weak, their firepower is poor and their equipment is poor. An example of this is that an American infantry unit cannot take or destroy a machine gun position in a properly prepared bunker except by calling for air and artillery; however, the NVA can destroy any American bunker with B40 or B-41 (RPG) rockets.[2]

While this statement is debatable, it certainly reflects confidence by PLAF and PAVN officers in their equipment and in their ability to complete their missions. The same confidence was shown by communist POWs surveyed by the US Army in 1965: 94 percent of them expressed satisfaction in their own equipment.[3]

While the division itself was a recent creation, its organic regiments – the 271st, 272nd and 273rd – had been operating in South Vietnam for several years. While all the regiments and the whole division were officially part of the ostensibly South Vietnamese NLF, the troops themselves were a mixture of local recruits, 'regrouped' Southerners[4] and North Vietnamese regulars. The official divisional history is quite clear on that:

> [S]erving in the ranks of the 9th Division were cadres of combatants from all parts of the country. Many cadres born in the South or

A group of NLF members posing for a photo. Note the combination of weapons, including an RPG-2 rocket launcher. While inaccurate, unreliable, and often poorly deployed, the RPG-2 was the basic anti-tank and support weapon of both PAVN and PLAF. Not only was it used against allied armoured vehicles, but also as an infantry support weapon when assaulting trench lines or bunkers. (Albert Grandolini)

A selection of heavier infantry weapons on display. From left to right two Soviet RPDs, an old Second World War-vintage US-made Browning Automatic Rifle, and a ubiquitous 60mm mortar, based on the French Brandt design. (Albert Grandolini).

familiar with the southern theatre had been organized into main force regiments in the North and then dispatched to the southern theatre. There were young people who, driven by hatred for the US-puppet clique, had grown up in the concerted uprising movements in their localities and then joined the Liberation Army. There were also cadres who had set foot on the land of eastern Nam Bo for the first time.[5]

Leaving aside the rhetoric and propaganda, this is an admission that the 9th Division was a composite unit comprised of regiments originally organised and trained in the North. To a certain extent, the division was an expeditionary force not dissimilar from its American opponents. Even the habit of replacing losses with local recruits (when available) and conscripts from North Vietnam was remarkably similar to American practice.

The first and oldest regiment of the 9th Division was the 271st Regiment, which was officially created on 9 February 1961 in Tay Ninh Province. Initially, it only comprised a single battalion, formed and trained in Xuan Mai, Ha Dong, North Vietnam, and infiltrated south on what would become the Ho Chi Minh Trail. According to the 9th Division's history, the trek took two months and 27 days.[6] A second battalion was added in September, probably mixing northern cadres with local recruits. The third battalion appeared in June 1963. The 271st held the distinction of being the first PLAF regiment operating in War Zone D and the first full unit redeployed from the North to the South. Before the forming of the 9th Division in 1965, it operated as an independent unit. It took part in the Dong Xoai operation in 1965: tasked with ambushing ARVN reinforcements, it was not engaged because no ARVN troops came through its ambush zone. After that, it was the first regiment of the 9th Division to engage US Army units in the battle for Hill 65 in November 1965.

The 272nd Regiment was the second-oldest PLAF main force regiment, being created on 22 December 1961 at Xuan Mai (DRV). Regimental command and one battalion, the 6th, left North Vietnam in the same month, heading south. This advanced guard was in South Vietnam by March 1962. The two other organic infantry battalions (the 5th and 4th) also reached South Vietnam in the same year. The 272nd was officially established in War Zone D in June 1962 and, like its older counterpart, operated as an independent unit until the formation of the 9th PLAF Division. In June 1965, the regiment attacked the ARVN base at Dong Xoai, inflicting severe losses on the South Vietnamese. While the regiment heralded the battle as a great victory, as usual with the 9th Division's claims, the truth was somewhat different. The attack by the 272nd against the post of Dong Xoai did inflict severe losses on the defenders, but they were able to hold their positions. The episode prompted General Westmoreland to request authorisation to employ US units, in this case the 173rd Airborne Brigade, in a direct combat role. Although the request was granted, the deployment of the airborne troops did not happen, postponing the 'official' combat debut of US Army units by several weeks. USAF air support was instead liberally applied, causing significant losses to the 272nd and the other 9th Division regiments involved in the action.

The last organic regiment of the 9th Division was the 273rd Regiment. Differently from the other two regiments, the units were not formed in the North and then infiltrated to the South, but raised in South Vietnam. The decision to create the regiment was, in all

Another common support weapon, the Soviet SG-43 or its Chinese copy, the Type 53. It was seen with shielded (as in this case) and unshielded mounts. It was reasonably portable and provided a high volume of fire. (Albert Grandolini)

PLAF troops on the attack. The photo is possibly staged but highlights the way the SG-43 could be quickly moved while in the attack. In the centre of the picture a soldier is carrying the wheeled mount while behind him, on the right of the picture another is carrying the weapon itself. (Albert Grandolini)

ikelihood, taken in early 1964,[7] and it started forming in July or August of the same year. MACV sources identified the first two battalions, designated T80 and T70, in Tay Ninh Province in this timeframe. The third battalion, 263 Dong Thap, appeared in December. The regiment was officially activated on 22 December 1964, in Base Area 357. The battalions were not local of the area. Battalion T80 – renamed the 1st Battalion 273rd Regiment, and then the 7th Battalion – was one of the oldest Viet Cong units, having been formed in the Mekong Delta region in 1959. Battalion T70 was created from cadres of Battalion T80 in 1962, again in the delta region. Battalion 263 also came from the delta region, having been formed in Khien Hoa Province in 1963. Officers and NCOs were 'regroupees' from the North, while the rank and file were local sympathisers.[8] It was originally a local unit, raised to the status of main force unit before being transferred to Tay Ninh to create the 273rd Regiment. Its first outing was the Dong Xoai campaign, where it suffered heavy losses from air attacks in exchange for a marginal role in the whole operation.

The 9th Division was commanded by Senior Colonel Hoang Cam. A northerner and a career PAVN officer, he had assumed command of the division upon its establishment. He brought with him a supposedly considerable military experience. Having joined the Viet Minh in 1945 as a simple private, he experienced a meteoric rise in the ranks during the First Indochina War. By 1954, he was commanding the 209th Regiment of the 312th Division at Dien Bien Phu, where, according to the 9th Division's history, he personally captured General De Castries, the French garrison's commander.[9] After 1954, Cam's career was typical of a promising officer, with staff and field assignments culminating in the command of the 312th Division. In January 1965, he was sent to South Vietnam, where he became an ardent proponent of big unit battles and was often outspoken in his confidence in the division's ability to defeat American forces.

101st PAVN Infantry Regiment

For ATTLEBORO, B-2 Front added the 101st Infantry Regiment to the 9th Division. The 101st was a regular PAVN formation raised and trained in the DRV and then deployed to South Vietnam in early 1966 as part of the 7th PAVN Division. MACV intelligence started to report the regiment north of Saigon in April–May of the same year. On paper, the regiment was organised like others in the 9th PLAF Division, but for ATTLEBORO it appears to have been much closer to its paper strength than its compatriots. This can be deduced from the fact that General Thanh, the commander of B-2 Front, had used it to reinforce the 9th Division. Cam's division had suffered considerable losses in the previous months, and the regiment was seen as a fresh unit, as evinced by its role as the main effort in the operation.[10] The fact that it was a reasonably fresh unit can also be inferred by the oblique reference to it in Cam's assessment that it had seen few combats and was relatively inexperienced.[11] During ATTLEBORO, the 101st Regiment would be reinforced by anti-aircraft units and a mortar company from the 9th Division, bringing its effective strength to around 3,000 troops.

3
THE US ARMY IN VIETNAM

By October 1966, major US units had been deployed in Vietnam for more than a year. Starting with the landing of US Marine Corps battalions in Da Nang in March 1965, more and more units had poured in the country. By the start of Operation ATTLEBORO, there were two US Army and one USMC corps-sized formations active in Vietnam. The original two Marine battalions had become many dozens of US Army, USMC, Korean and Australian battalions. More were still coming: peak allied troop strength would not be reached until the summer and autumn of 1968. There was also the South Vietnamese Army that, notwithstanding its weaknesses and faults, was carrying as much of the fighting as it could. Yet ATTLEBORO involved almost only US Army and US Air Force units, so this chapter will focus on them rather than be a generic description of the whole allied war effort.

Describing the US Army that fought the Vietnam War is a complex task. This has often produced caricatured and skewered portraits, emphasising specific agendas or resting on incorrect assumptions. In large part this is because the US Army that deployed in Vietnam was itself a complex entity. Certainly, there is a significant amount of truth in the assertion that Vietnam was one of the few wars the US military entered prepared for. On the other hand, in 1965, the US Army was just emerging from a round of changes and adaptation. The US Army formations that fought during Operation ATTLEBORO were the product of President Eisenhower's relative neglect of conventional forces and of President Kennedy's sudden surge of interest in them. They were also the last formations that America drafted into a war. Yet this is also a misleading image. Drafted or not, it was an army that possessed a strong core of long-term professional and motivated soldiers at all levels and ranks. Contrary to the popular, and wholly inaccurate, perception of an army of clueless draftees coming from minorities and lower classes sent to fight an unpopular war, the US Army stepped into Vietnam with confidence and was prepared for the struggle. According to US Department of Defense statistics, of the 2,590,000 men and women who served in South Vietnam, less than 25 percent were draftees. It is worth noting that in the Second World War, that figure was 66 percent. Some 79 percent of the servicemen sent to Vietnam had completed high school. Minorities were represented, as they were in US society at large: African-Americans comprised 10.6 percent of the men actually serving 'in country', and made up 13.5 percent of the US population at the time. It was not the caricatured army portrayed by some sources.

It was also not an army blinded by an obsession with a conventional war in Germany. Chapter 1 has already discussed the views of General Westmoreland on the war in Vietnam and US COIN doctrine. Furthermore, he and his command were braced for a long struggle. There was no reference to a quick victory. The decision to introduce US combat troops had been taken reflecting this view. While there were hopes that a show of force and determination could have restrained Hanoi, it was not part of US Army policy. This expectation of a prolonged struggle led to the first characterising element of the US Army in the Vietnam War: the concept of 'tour of duty'. Soldiers were not left with their units for the duration of the war, as they had been during the Second World War except for transfers, promotions or incapacitation. Differently from what had been seen in contemporary 'long wars', and unlike the approach used in Vietnam by the Australian Army, US units were not rotated in their entirety.

The tour of duty was both a choice and a necessity. Replacements would have been needed anyway, as units struggled to maintain their authorised strength through combat losses, normal rotations, temporary assignments and regular attrition due to accident and sickness. Rotating whole units would have been expensive and unwieldy, and would have increased the strain on the whole army. The US Army had to maintain its worldwide presence and deterrence, notwithstanding its commitment to South East Asia. Korea had to be defended and stabilised. Kim Il Sung was again heating up his confrontation with South Korea, and the new government in Seoul, head by General Park, was still consolidating its power and its military. West Germany and NATO could not be left alone, and neither could Japan. The potential for other crises did not diminish just because Vietnam had heated up, so a strategic reserve had to be maintained

The tip of the US Army's spear. Here Sgt William H. Mcmullen of the 1-16th Infantry Regiment, 1st Infantry Division, wades through a jungle stream near Bien Hoa on 7 August 1965. Note he is carrying an M14 rifle. The 1st Infantry Division would not receive the new M16 until 1966. (US Army)

Vietnam was also not the only concomitant contingency mission: United States troops had also deployed to the Dominican Republic in 1965, and their mission was not yet completed.

The supporters of rotating whole units never explained how the US Army could have maintained its global active presence with such a policy. While on a purely numerical basis it could have been possible, that did not consider the need for pre-deployment training and acclimatisation to Vietnam. Simply taking infantry battalions from southern Germany for Vietnam duty would not have been possible or even advisable. Rotating whole units was probably impossible, especially considering the administration's decision to not mobilise reserve components. Without such deployment, even maintaining the proposed build-up in Vietnam and global readiness would have been extremely difficult, as hinted by the US Army Chief of Staff, General Harold K. Johnson.[1]

Beside these strictures, there was also the will to keep the deployed force as strong and cohesive as possible. While this could appear in contrast with the tour of duty policy, it was not. First of all, it placed less burden on the individual. As Westmoreland himself articulated, the one-year tour ensured US troops remained relatively fresh.[2] Thus, the tour of duty was seen as a positive element despite the post-war criticism. Individual replacements avoided the wholesale rotation of command staff at unit and formation level. While individual officers rotated home or were assigned to other duties, there was always a core of people to assure continuity. Veterans trained newcomers, rather than whole units having to adapt to the field, a phenomenon decried in more recent wars in Iraq and Afghanistan. Individual replacements would still have been necessary if a unit rotation policy was implemented. Despite rotating whole battalions rather than individuals, the Australian Army was still forced to send a constant stream of individual replacements to just keep the deployed units up to strength. The Australians also had the luxury of being able to focus almost their whole effort on maintaining a single brigade in Vietnam.

One-year tours ensured the US Army was able to maintain its global presence along with a reasonably effective combat force in Vietnam. While there are plenty of anecdotal accounts of poorly trained replacements, drafts sent to Vietnam did complete courses at the Jungle Warfare Training establishment at Fort Polk, Louisiana, before deployment, and divisions in Vietnam maintained training centres to ensure the constant stream of replacements was prepared for combat. Tales of unprepared replacements were common in the Second World War and the Korean War. Considering the scale of the deployment, the lack of reserve mobilisation and the acceptance of a prolonged permanence in Vietnam, coupled with a constantly active theatre, despite its potential shortcomings the system was, on balance, the only one suited to the context.

Organisation

Numbers, draftees versus professionals and the one-year tours are only one facet of the US Army deployment to Vietnam. Organisation is another. The units deploying to Vietnam in 1965 and 1966 were part of an army in transition. As already mentioned, the US Army had just emerged from a period of change. This reorganisation process had not been as smooth as numbers or Tables of Organisation and Equipment appear to tell. The net effect of overreliance on nuclear weapons during Eisenhower's first mandate was that divisions and brigades had been disbanded or reduced. While the process had been slowed or halted during his second term in office, it had not really been reversed until a new administration took over in 1961. In 1965, Kennedy's increased funding and Secretary of Defense McNamara's determination to provide a valid alternative to nuclear weapons were just starting to take effect. As far the US Army was concerned, the main legacy of Eisenhower's years was the Pentomic or Pentatomic divisional organisation, a plan to structure infantry divisions around five battle groups plus supports, each battle group in turn comprising five companies and their support. These units should have not only been able to disperse in event of nuclear attack, but to dominate the battlefield through their own nuclear weapons. The embodiment of these concepts was the Davy Crockett Atomic Recoilless Rifle, a weapon whose warhead blast radius was greater than its range.

The idea proved an organisational disaster but was officially discarded only in 1963. Thus, the US Army had only two years to reinvent itself with a new structure. ROAD, the Reorganisation Objective Army Division, was, by circumstances, a throwback to principles developed in the Second World War and Korea, with some concessions to improvements in command and control technology and helicopters. Divisions again had nine battalions, in a mix of infantry, armour and mechanized infantry suitable for their assigned missions. The battalions were not assigned to fixed regiments, but directly to the division, while retaining a regimental designation for historical purposes. In turn, the division had three brigade headquarters that would exercise control in the field. ROAD discarded a new infantry division concept to adapt the armored division combat command that was already flexible and effective, as recognised even by the proponents of the Pentomic concept, to infantry divisions. It was a sound common sense approach. The divisions had their own integral armored cavalry squadron (battalion-size) and four artillery battalions, three equipped with the workhorse of the US Army, the 105mm M101 howitzer, and the other having a mix of 155mm and 8-in (203mm) howitzers. The 155mm guns in infantry divisions were usually towed, while the 8-in howitzer could be towed or self-propelled, the latter the fearsome M110. A new addition to the division was an organic aviation element in the shape of the helicopter.

Helicopters became a centrepiece of the US Army's modernisation, with a fully airmobile division being created, first with the 11th Air Assault Division to test the concept, and then the famous 1st Cavalry Division to implement it in Vietnam. Later, the 101st Airborne Division was also reconfigured as an airmobile formation. Air mobility was not just restricted to transport functions, as combat helicopters were also developed and deployed. Organic divisional helicopter units were supplemented by a considerable number of independent battalions, sometimes even brigades, designed to increase the number of available helicopters and enable even non-airmobile divisions to enjoy a significant degree of helicopter capability. Transport helicopters and gunships were to become an important fixture in almost all engagements in Vietnam. In this regard, the US Army was particularly fortunate in having two excellent platforms: the light UH-1 and the heavier CH-47. Both these turbine-powered helicopters proved critical workhorses throughout the conflict and are still in use in the early 21st century in the United States military and across the world.

The final innovation in the US Army was the new Separate Infantry Brigades, which were raised from 1965 as a direct answer to the growing commitment in Vietnam. They were outside the usual divisional structure and were designed to be part of a newly organised strategic reserve to enable the US Army to respond to unforeseen crises while its divisions were either already forward-deployed or earmarked for such deployment. This was seen as a cheap way to offset the build-up. These brigades comprised three standard or light infantry battalions, one 105mm artillery battalion and one cavalry troop. These combat units contained the usual service units, but on a smaller scale than a traditional division. With commitments to the

Republic of Vietnam constantly increasing, all these units ended being deployed to the theatre, completely nullifying their intended role.

Infantry Battalions

In 1965, US battalions – be they infantry, armored or mechanized – were standardised on a triangular organisation of three line companies and a large Headquarters and Headquarters Company (HHC). In turn, the three rifle companies comprised three infantry platoons and one heavy weapons platoon. The Headquarters Company controlled both the administrative echelon of the battalion (logistic, administrative, communications and medical) and its surveillance and heavy weapons assets. The latter comprised a mortar platoon with four 4.2-in (107mm) mortars and an anti-tank (AT) platoon with three 106mm recoilless rifles (RCLs). Surveillance and reconnaissance was provided by a radar platoon equipped with ground surveillance radar for counter-battery purposes, and a reconnaissance platoon with one scout squad (12 enlisted men and four M60 light machine guns), one infantry squad (10 men with one M60) and an AT section with eight men serving two 106mm RCLs.

The infantry platoon was, on paper, composed of a small command team, three 10-man rifle squads and one 11-man weapons squad. The weapons squad pooled all the platoon heavy weapons, namely two M60 light machine guns and two M67 90mm RCLs. The rifle squads had only assault rifles and two M79 hand-held grenade launchers. This organisation had been designed when the standard rifle of the US Army was the 7.62mm M14. While the M14 was capable of fully automatic fire, the standard infantry version was not supposed to be used in that way. Each squad received two specially configured M14 automatic rifles, with full auto setting enabled and a bipod. While several units deployed to Vietnam with the M14, that rifle had, officially, already been superseded by the newer M16 and M16A1, a new, plastic, 5.56mm assault rifle. The M16 was by default configured to allow automatic fire and thus led to the disappearance of the dedicated automatic riflemen for squads so equipped. The infantry company also included a weapons platoon with two 106mm RCLs and three 81mm mortars.

Mechanized Units

One of the most enduring clichés about Vietnam is the war being an infantry and helicopter war. While images of helicopters and troops walking in the jungle abound, armoured and mechanized vehicles are strangely absent, except in specialised publications. This is particularly striking considering that three tank battalions, at least seven armored cavalry squadrons (three with the 11th Armored Cavalry Regiment) and eight mechanized infantry battalions served in Vietnam with the US Army. Tanks were the 90mm-armed M48A3, while the majority of mechanized infantry vehicles were M113s in various different guises.

Organisationally, tank battalions deployed with three tank companies, each with three five-tank platoons, and two tanks for the company commander and his executive officer, making 17 tanks in all. Two more tanks were in the HHC, supported by self-propelled 4.2-in mortars on M113s (M106 mortar carriers) and a plethora of support vehicles. Scouts were mounted on M113 armoured personnel carriers (APCs), and the ubiquitous 106mm RCLs were mounted on jeeps.

Mechanized infantry battalions had three companies organised as standard infantry units, but with the addition of four M113 APCs

A fine study of a 1st Infantry Division instructor demonstrating proper operations of the M16 in 1968. By then the reliability problems that plagued the initial issues of the weapon had been largely solved. Still, proper weapons training was critically important. All US Army Divisions maintained combat schools for replacements in Vietnam. (US Army)

US Army combat units replaced their M14 rifles with the new M16s during 1965 and 1966. Here replacements for the 1st Infantry Division are training with M16 rifles at Lai Khe in 1968. (US Army)

and their .50-cal heavy machine guns. The 81mm mortars of the mortar platoon were carried on modified M113s (M125 mortar carriers) and the 106mm RCLs on jeeps. The HHC had the same organisation as that of the tank battalion but replaced the two M48 tanks with M577 command vehicles, another variant of the ubiquitous M113. Furthermore, the HHC had two M132s, a flamethrower-vehicle based on the M113.

While the war had always been seen as an infantryman's war, the US Army made significant use of its armoured and mechanized forces. Here a fine study of a 1st Infantry Division M113 in ACAV configuration, with a shielded cupola for the commander's M2 heavy machine gun, and two shielded M60 light machine guns, one per side. (US Army)

Armored Cavalry Squadrons were a different beast. They were full combined arms battalion-sized units grouping tanks, mechanized vehicles and helicopters. They comprised four company-sized Troops, three armored and one air-mounted. The three Armored Troops comprised a small HQ section, with five M113s and one M732 recovery vehicle, and three Cavalry Platoons, each with two M48 tanks, one M125 mortar carrier, six M113s and one infantry squad. The Air Cavalry Troop had one Scout Platoon with five or six helicopters (originally OH-13s, then OH-6s and OH-58s), an Aero Weapons Platoon with five or six UH-1-based gunships and an Aero Rifle Platoon with another five UH-1s and an infantry element with four nine-man squads, each with one M60 machine gun and two M79 grenade launchers. The Squadron also had a Headquarters and Headquarters Troop assuring command, logistic and support functions. This HHT also included a section with four M132 flamethrower vehicles. The cavalry squadron was thus a powerful and flexible unit. The three squadrons that were part of the 11th Armored Cavalry Regiment were organised on different lines, but as they did not participate in Operation ATTLEBORO, they will not be discussed here.

The US Army deployed only 90mm-armed M48 gun tanks to Vietnam, not their heavier and newer M60 offspring with their 105mm gun. Here an M48A3 from 1-4th Cav, 1st Infantry Division, moves through the jungle. (US Army)

Nevertheless, the Vietnam War's realities and practical lessons led to several alterations to this approach. While mechanized units did not experience the same level of change as regular infantry, they did adapt their equipment and organisation to the situation in Vietnam. The most visible change was the introduction of yet another variant of the M113, the M113 ACAV (Armored Cavalry Assault Vehicle). The M113 was first fielded

Elements of the 1-4th Cav with M48s and an M113. Note the dismounted troopers still carry M14 rifles. (US Army Cav)

in Vietnam by the ARVN in its basic troop carrier version, equipped with a single .50-cal M2 heavy machine gun mounted on the front of the commander's cupola. The vehicle was extremely well received thanks to its astonishing mobility, even in the Mekong Delta area in the wet season, and its firepower. Yet the vehicle had its limitations, some inherent to its design but others to its employment in Vietnam. The vehicle was designed for American-size infantrymen, and one of the most evident drawbacks of its ARVN service was the need for track commanders to completely expose themselves to fire the cupola-mounted M2 machine gun. When the 'terror' effect of the vehicle wore off and the Viet Cong found ways to deal with them, the exposed nature of its main weapon led to significant casualties in vehicle commanders, most notably at the battle of Ap Bac in 1963. The other significant limitation was the lack of provision for mounted combat. The M113 had been designed as a battle taxi, with transported infantry supposed to dismount before contact. In Vietnam, ARVN officers and their American advisors found it more expedient to continue assaults while mounted, reducing infantry vulnerability and increasing the shock effect. Yet the only way for embarked troops to fire was to open the roof hatch, climb onto the vehicle and fire from an exposed position.

ARVN officers and US advisors ended up field-modifying the M113, attaching extra weapons on the roof sides and adding shields to them and the main .50-cal machine gun. Initial efforts were crude – the first vehicles thus modified received shields made from discarded boiler plates or ship hulls – but effective. In turn, this led to the US Army Pacific developing kits with side and front shields to apply to the M113 commander's cupola, transforming it into a sort of turret. These kits were installed in US Army workshops in Okinawa. These efforts also spurred a definitive solution in the US, with FMC manufacturing kits with better all-around protection for the makeshift turret and better shields for the M60. This in turn led to the transformation of the M113 from a simple battle taxi to a full-fledged combat vehicle. While on paper ACAVs should have been restricted to cavalry units, they found use in mechanized infantry battalions too. Their combat use was studied and sanctioned by MACV through its Mechanized and Combat Operation in Vietnam (MACOV) report, published in 1967.

The introduction of ACAV vehicles also transformed the mechanized infantry platoons. While indented to move on tracks and fight dismounted, in Vietnam they found it increasingly expedient to fight while mounted. Squad organisation dissolved and was replaced by a track organisation. Each vehicle was now the primary sub-unit of the platoon and the infantrymen became track crews, manning the additional machine guns, supplying ammunition to the gunners and, on relevant occasions, using their M79 grenade launchers from the now open troop compartment.

Cavalry units discarded their M114 scout vehicles even before shipping to Vietnam. Trials in Vietnam had proved the vehicles a massive failure. Underpowered, possessing limited cross-country capability and barely amphibious, the 'little brothers' of the M113 were quietly removed from units. One wonders why these obvious deficiencies were not discovered in testing…

Artillery

Thankfully for military historians, wargamers and modellers, the 1960s and 1970s were a period when the US Army's artillery was organised in an extremely standardised fashion. Notwithstanding equipment or affiliation, all artillery battalions followed the same organisational pattern, with one Headquarters and Headquarters Service Battery (HHSB) and three firing batteries with six guns each. There were only two exceptions: heavy divisional battalions had three basic firing batteries and one additional battery with four 8-in self-propelled howitzers, while heavy SP batteries were equipped with 175mm or 8-in SP howitzers that possessed four guns rather than six. From an organisational standpoint, the whole system was exceedingly simple and standardised. The HHSB comprised both the battalion HQ and the battalion fire direction center. It also included the communication and liaison elements of the battalion, namely the Forward Observers Team that in turn were attached to infantry and armored battalions. This standardisation survived the war largely intact, with almost no alteration except the merging of 8-in and 175mm SP units in composite battalions, as the guns were, as will be later discussed, interchangeable.

Behind this standardisation of battalions there was a panoply of weapons and attachments. Broadly speaking, artillery battalions were either divisional (for separate brigades, brigaded) or independent. The formers were organic to the divisions. Each division had three 105mm howitzer battalions and one heavy battalion with three 155mm howitzer batteries, and one battery with four 8-in self-propelled M110s. Independent battalions ranged from 105mm howitzers to 8-in SP guns, with 155mm towed or SP howitzers and 175mm SP guns in the middle. Theoretically, independent battalions were subordinated to artillery groups and the groups to corps, but in Vietnam the corps echelon was replaced by the Field Forces. While divisional battalions provided direct support to the division's brigades, the artillery group and their component battalions were attached to divisions and brigades for specific operations, the longer-ranged guns being able to support even multiple operations at once. The system allowed Field Force and division commanders extreme flexibility and, coupled with air mobility and long ranges, ensured plenty of fire support available to all units in the field.

During the whole Vietnam War, 29 independent artillery battalions deployed to Vietnam. To be more specific, the II FFV (Field Force, Vietnam) artillery in 1966 controlled two artillery groups – the 23rd and 54th – the latter being deployed in October that year. The two groups together controlled eight battalions, the overwhelming majority with the 23rd.

The workhorse of the US artillery was the Second World War-vintage M2A1/M101 105mm howitzer. Here an example from B Battery, 3-319th Artillery assigned to the 173rd Airborne Brigade fires at an enemy position in October 1965. (US Army)

In 1966 the venerable M101 started to be replaced by the new, lightweight, M102 105mm howitzer. The gun is from the same battery of 3-319th Artillery. (US Army)

The workhorse of the divisional artillery was the 105mm M101A1 howitzer. A familiar sight from 1942's Operation TORCH onward, the M101 had been the mainstay of the US Army's artillery from 1940. Originally called the M2A1, in 1962 the name was changed to M101A1. With a range of 11,000 metres, a sustained rate of fire of three rounds per minute and a maximum of 30 rounds per minute in the first three minutes of firing, it was an effective weapon. It was also a weapon that was easy to maintain and move. Its weight of 4,980lb allowed both towing on primitive roads and deployment via CH-47 helicopters. In March 1966, a new 105mm gun, the M102, was introduced to Vietnam. It was lighter, newer and added another 500 metres to its range, conserving the M101's rate of fire. One of the big advantages of the new gun was that it only required a ¾-ton truck as prime mover, compared to 2½-tons for the M101. While the M101 was a very conventional design, with split trail and shield, the M102 had an open box trail and when emplaced was jacked on a firing platform, allowing for a faster 360-degree traverse. The 105mm gun was supplement by another Second World War veteran, the M114A1 155mm howitzer. Adopted by the US Army in 1941 as the M1A1, its name changed during the sweeping renaming campaign led by McNamara in 1962, as with the M2 (it was also when USAF Phantoms were renamed from F-110 to F-4). The M114A1 was a heavier weapon, at 12,950lb, almost thrice that of the M101. It had to be towed by a 5-ton truck and airlifting required not even a CH-47, but a specialised CH-54. Its range was a respectable 14,600 metres but with a reduced rate of fire due to a heavier shell. While its initial rate of fire was 12 rounds per minute, after three minutes it dropped to just one round. However, its rounds were more powerful than those of the 105mm: a single 155mm round's impact area was 360 metres in radius compared to 175 metres for the 105mm. A special flechette round was developed for the 155mm howitzer. Carrying several small steel darts inside a case shot, it made a fearsome direct-fire munition against infantry.

Aviation Units

Together with artillery, aviation was the main force multiplier the US Army enjoyed in Vietnam. Be they gunships, transports or command and control 'ships', helicopters were a mainstay of the US effort in the theatre. Helicopters came early with the advisors and, captured in iconic images, evacuated the last US officials and civilians from the

Infantrymen of 2-14th Infantry Regiment, 25th Infantry Division, deploys from their UH-1D during a search and destroy operation in May 1966. (US Army)

roof of Saigon's US Embassy in 1975. While the use of helicopters in combat was nothing new, having been pioneered by the USMC in Korea and by the French in Algeria, the scale of their use was unprecedented. Technically speaking, after several less-than-promising starts, the US Army fielded two very capable workhorses by 1965, the Bell UH-1 Huey and the Boeing-Vertol CH-47 Chinook.

Yet despite enduring images, helicopters were not omnipresent in the US Army, neither at home nor in Vietnam. Being a new, expensive and maintenance-intensive component of the US Army force structure, they were deployed in Vietnam in relatively few units. Only two divisions, the famed 1st Cavalry and the 101st Airborne, enjoyed full helicopter support. The other divisions had a single organic aviation battalion, comprising one assault company equipped with around 25 UH-1s and one general service company with light observation helicopters (initially Bell OH-13s) and four OV-1 Mohawk fixed-wing aircraft. The Hueys in the assault company could be configured for different roles, including armed missions, but at times a platoon of UH-1B dedicated gunships was attached to the company.

The majority of aviation assets came from independent battalions, either permanently attached to a specific division or operating under control of the Aviation Brigade and its component groups supporting a specific Field Force. In turn, the battalions comprised independent aviation companies assigned according to their needs. Aviation companies could be aerial weapons, gunships or airmobile (light) with UH-1s, or medium transport equipped with CH-47s. This flexible organisation was designed to ensure combat units in the field received constant and appropriate support, while maintenance duties were carried by larger organisations properly supplied.

The workhorse of the whole helicopter fleet was the Bell UH-1. A recent design at the time, it is widely considered one of the most capable light transport helicopters ever made. The most common variant used in Vietnam was the UH-1D. Introduced in 1963, it was a stretched and uprated version of the UH-1B variant, designed to accommodate a full infantry squad of 11 men in its troop compartment. In 1965 and 1966, it provided the majority of troop transport missions. It could be armed with two 7.62mm M60 light machine guns firing from the troop compartment. Supplementing the UH-1D 'slick' there were the UH-1B and UH-1C variants. Originally procured as a troop transport, the UH-1B was the first Huey variant to serve in Vietnam, usually in an armed configuration. By 1965, it was supplement by the UH-1C version with uprated engine. The UH-1C was the first variant specifically designed as a gunship. With a maximum speed of 140 knots, the gunship could carry different weapon packages. A common configuration was one or two forward-firing 7.62mm machine guns, either single or rotary, and a pair of rocket pods. Often, two M60 machine guns were carried in the troop compartment, with associated gunners, to provide coverage of the side and rear arcs. Some Hueys even had a chin turret with a 40mm automatic grenade launcher.

Supplementing the Hueys was the heavier Boeing-Vertol CH-47 Chinook. The Chinook had been designed as a medium cargo helicopter, hence the 'C' designation. It sported an impressive cargo capacity of 33 equipped troops, one 105mm howitzer or a light vehicle slung underneath its fuselage. It was also a troubled helicopter. It first arrived in Vietnam in 1965 with the 1st Cavalry Division in its CH-47A version. While the US Army had great hopes for the Chinook, being a recent addition to the helicopter stable it was still suffering from teething problems. Originally, what would become the CH-47 was just an enlarged version of the Vertol Model 107, the CH-46 used by the US Navy and US Marine Corps (along with foreign operators). The Vertol Company had proposed its Model 107 to the US Army in 1959, but it was rejected as too small. Further design effort led to the Model 114, that was accepted first as the YCH-1B (YCH-1A being the prototype designation of the Model 107) in 1961. In 1962, it was redesigned as CH-47A, Boeing having in the meantime acquired Vertol and set up the Boeing-Vertol division. With the first production examples reaching units in late 1962, the CH-47 did not benefit from the same extensive tests and trials the UH-1 received. As a result, when the CH-47A was deployed to Vietnam it was found to be underpowered, its two turbines being excessively affected by heat and humidity. It also required extensive maintenance. It was not unheard of for 50 percent of Chinooks in an aviation company to be under maintenance and unflyable at one time. Improved versions would follow in 1967 and 1968, but for the first two years of the war, the CH-47A soldiered on. Despite its teething problems, the Chinooks gave the US Army the ability to quickly lift whole artillery batteries to locations away from the road network, and to keep them supplied.

US Army major formations involved in ATTLEBORO

The 196th Light Infantry Brigade (Separate)

While the brunt of the fighting would be borne by battalions from the 1st and 25th Infantry Divisions, ATTLEBORO is usually associated with the 196th Light Infantry Brigade. This brigade was a recently raised formation and did not share the storied past of the two divisions. It had been formed in 1965 as the first light infantry brigade of the US Army under the ROAD structure. Four light infantry brigades were planned to create a new strategic reserve in view of the increased overseas commitments, such as in Vietnam. The formation was officially activated on 15 September 1965. The brigade itself was formed by taking over the remnant of the 2nd Brigade, 5th Infantry Division, and adding more newly organised infantry battalions. Basically, it was created from scratch using new recruits. At full strength it included three infantry battalions: the 2nd Battalion, 1st Infantry; the 3rd Battalion, 21st Infantry; and the 4th Battalion, 41st Infantry. These three battalions were to be supported by an armored cavalry troop, F Troop, 17th Cavalry, and the 3rd Battalion, 82nd Artillery, the latter equipped with 105mm howitzers. Engineer, signal, support and public information companies, plus other detachments, completed the formation. The 196th Brigade's commanding officer was Colonel Francis S. Conaty.

Organising and training the brigade itself was a complex endeavour that took time. Originally cantoned at Fort Devens, Massachusetts, the brigade had to send detachments to Camp Edwards near Cape Cod to exploit the local training facilities, due to a lack of such facilities at Camp Edwards. Training was further hampered by a scarcity of qualified officers and NCOs; three groups of them, totalling 120 key individuals, were transferred out of the brigade to strengthen other deploying units in 1965.[3] In December 1965, barely three months into its existence, the 196th was secretly alerted for deployment overseas to the Dominican Republic. The Secretary of Defense wanted it to replace elements of the 82nd Airborne Division currently deployed there on peacekeeping operations. The US Army wanted the paratroopers back in their role as strategic reserve. While the brigade was by no means ready, the mission was – at least on paper – not an overwhelmingly difficult one. Peacekeeping operations in the Dominican Republic were not a frontline combat mission. The target date for the deployment was 15 July 1966. A final exercise with the whole formation was performed at Camp Drum, New York, on 30 March. With support from US Special Forces, the formation trained in low-intensity counterinsurgency, security and riot control operations in preparation for the Caribbean deployment.[4] The 196th returned to its new home of Fort Stevens on 17 May, with embarkation plans for the Caribbean completed by 23 June. Only one week before embarkation, the Secretary of Defense decided the brigade was not needed in the Dominican Republic, instead offering it to MACV, and on 24 June, the 196th Light Infantry Brigade was officially ordered to Vietnam. This sparked additional training, a switch from M14 battle rifles to M16 assault rifles and a new set of movement plans.

The main body of the brigade left Boston on 15 July and arrived in Vietnam a month later, disembarking at Vung Tau. Jungle warfare training classes were conducted on the transports bound to Vietnam, with additional classes on weaponry and tactics.[5] Describing the 196th as a green unit would have been appropriate. In the month between leaving Boston and reaching Vietnam, MACV debated over its actual destination. Initially, it was envisioned as a security force in the Tuy Hoa area (I Field Force Vietnam, II ARVN Corps), but it was then marked for garrisoning Tay Ninh under the II FFV, in the III Corps Tactical Zone (III CTZ). With Westmoreland planning his season of

General Edward De Saussure, the controversial commander of the 196th Infantry Brigade, is pictured together with the Commander of South Korean Forces Vietnam, General Chae Myung Shin. (US Army)

major offensives to clear the area around Saigon first, the final location made perfect sense. If three new infantry and one artillery battalions seemed just a drop in the ocean, they were in addition to the whole 1st and 25th Infantry Divisions, part of the 9th Infantry Division, the 173rd Airborne Brigade, the 11th Armored Cavalry Regiment, the 199th Light Infantry Brigade and the Australian Task Force.

The 196th Light Infantry Brigade arrived at Vung Tau on 14 August with Colonel Conaty still at its helm. He was placed under operational control of the 25th Infantry Division and its commanding officer, General Weyand. Shortly after, Conaty was replaced by Brigadier General Edward H. De Saussure Jr. as Westmoreland had decided that every separate formation would have a general officer at the helm.[6] Conaty became De Saussure's deputy until an appropriate command position was found for him. While the 196th was new to Vietnam, De Saussure was not. Then aged 48, he had been Assistant Division Commander (Support) of the 25th Infantry Division for 15 months, four of them in Vietnam. De Saussure was an artilleryman by trade and a missile expert. Later in his career he would command the Army Missile Test Range at White Sands in New Mexico. While he had shown himself to be a capable administrator, he was neither an infantry officer nor a proven combat leader. In the 1940s, he had served with the 4th Field Artillery Battalion in the initial stages of the war in the Pacific but had then spent the rest of the war stateside. After 1945, he had served in staff and field artillery positions in the United States and Germany, being associated with missile developments. As far as infantry combat was concerned, he was as green as his brigade. On the other hand, he was assisted by Colonel Conaty, a career infantry officer who had led the 196th from its activation. Conaty thus

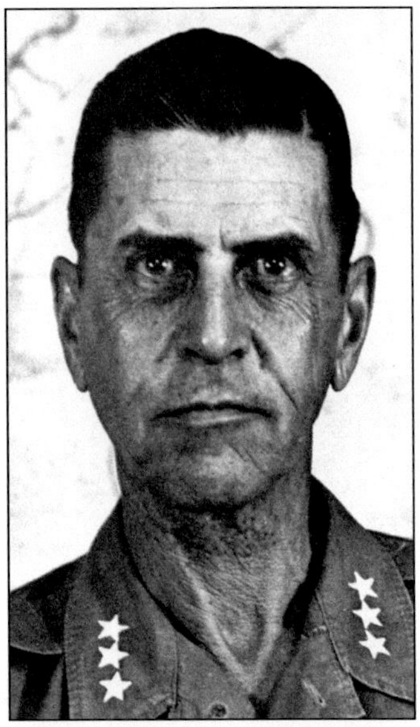

General Johnathan Seaman, the Commanding Officer of the 1st Infantry Division in 1965. He worked miracles to deploy his whole division to Vietnam despite conflicting orders and continual meddling from the Pentagon. (US Army)

knew the strengths and weaknesses of the formation and could advise De Saussure about infantry operations. In turn, De Saussure's previous Vietnam experience in the III CTZ should have provided a first-hand understanding of the peculiarity of the war in Vietnam and around Saigon. Consequently, at least on paper, the brigade had a capable command team.

1st Infantry Division, The Big Red One

While the 196th Brigade is usually associated with ATTLEBORO, the whole operation fell under the 1st Infantry Division and its commander at the time General DePuy. Several of its battalions were involved in fighting after the operation's first phase. As will be discussed later, the 1st Infantry Division also had a year-long series of battles against the 9th PLAF Division.

The 1st Infantry Division was, and still is, the oldest infantry division in the US Army. Formed in 1917, it was known as the Big Red One after its shoulder patch and boasted proud service in the Great War and the Second World War. In 1965, it was a ROAD division with two tank, two mechanized and seven standard infantry battalions stationed at Fort Riley, Kansas. Divisional units were the 1st Squadron, 4th Cavalry Regiment; the 1st Battalion, 5th Artillery (105mm); the 8th Battalion, 6th Artillery (155mm/8-in); the 1st Battalion, 7th Artillery (105mm); and the 2nd Battalion, 33rd Artillery (105mm). The aviation element was provided by the 1st Aviation Battalion. Medical, engineer, logistic, Military Police and assorted support units completed the division.

The 1st Division's involvement with Vietnam began on 14 April 1965 when its commander, General Jonathan O. Seaman, received secret orders to prepare plans for a brigade's deployment to South Vietnam within a month. Seaman ordered the 2nd Brigade, the division's rapid deployment unit, to prepare for the move. At the same time, he visited the Chief of Staff, General Johnson, in Washington to gather more information. At a meeting at the Pentagon on 22 April, Johnson told him: "Jack, the situation is getting real serious. And you better be prepared to send your division, or part of it, to Vietnam by 15 June."[7]

Further confirmation was received on 15 May, when the Army ordered Seaman to have the brigade personnel ready for movement, with a target date of 30 June. By the end of May, Vietnam was confirmed as the brigade's destination. Seaman and his staff worked feverishly to prepare the 2nd Brigade for deployment. The general was determined to have his best troops deploying for combat, even at the cost of cannibalising the rest of the 1st Division. Badly performing officers and NCOs from the three infantry battalions slated for deployment – the 2-16th, 1-18th and 2-18th Infantry – were replaced by high-performing personnel from other battalions. The same was done for the artillery battalion, the 1-7th Artillery, whose 105mm guns were supplemented by Battery C, 8-6th Artillery and its 155mm howitzers. Shortages in vehicles and equipment were filled by stripping the rest of the division. As Seaman later admitted, he was tearing the Big Red One apart to better prepare the 2nd Brigade. He rationalised this gamble with the fact that the 2nd Brigade was deploying without full divisional support, in a dangerous and fluid situation.[8]

The 2nd Brigade advance party deployed to Vietnam on 20 June by air, the bulk of the troops and equipment following by sea. The movement involved four ships, one for the troops and three for the equipment, and took from 25 June to 12 July, when the *General W.H. Gordon* reached Cam Ranh Bay. There, only one battalion disembarked, the 1-18th Infantry. The brigade was originally slated to protect the port installation at Qui Nhon, but MACV diverted it to Bien Hoa, on the outskirts of Saigon. The order only reached the 2nd Brigade after logistical arrangements for the previous location had already been made.[9] Thus, the *Gordon* continued to move to Vung Tau, were the rest of the troops disembarked, gathered their equipment, reached the local airfield and were flown to Bien Hoa, while the 1-18th protected the supply dump created for the brigade at Qui Nhon. Once in Vietnam, the 2nd Brigade started building a base and launched desultory clearing operations, all the while dealing with serious logistics problems. Food had to be provided by a US Navy Commissariat depot, and artillery ammunition by local ARVN units.

Meanwhile, back at Fort Riley, General Seaman had received orders to deploy the rest of the 1st Division to Vietnam. The orders specified a readiness date of 1 September or earlier. Seaman's gamble had come back to haunt him. The division was now short of officers, NCOs and specialists. On the other hand, non-deployable soldiers, usually personnel close to their discharge or transfer date, were plentiful. There were also shortcomings in equipment. According to US Army historian John Carland, the division had a shortage of approximately 250 officers and 3,000 enlisted men in July. Helicopter pilots were particularly scarce, many having been transferred to other units bound or already deployed to Vietnam, the 1st Cavalry Division being the prime culprit. Beside shortages, General Johnson, the Chief of Staff, also interfered with the division's organisation.

Johnson was not persuaded by the utility of mechanized vehicles in the jungles of Vietnam. Guided by his own experience in Korea, and a very superficial understanding of French mechanized operations during France's war against the Viet Minh, he was adamantly opposed to deploying mechanized forces there. More than French combat operations, what weighed heavily on Johnson's mind was Australian journalist Bernard Fall's appraisal of them. The latter's depiction of the destruction of GM 100 in the Central Highlands was prominent in American military appreciation.[10] Johnson thus not only demanded the removal of the two 1st Division tank battalions, but also the axing of its 8-in self-propelled howitzer battery. General Seaman opposed this decision. He stressed the need for the tanks and wanted at least one of the battalions deployed.

Johnson, however, was adamant in his opposition to tanks and offered the following views:

A. Korean experience demonstrated the ability of the oriental to employ relatively primitive but extremely effective box mines that defy detection. Effectiveness was especially good in areas where bottlenecks occurred on some routes. Our tanks had limited usefulness, although there are good examples of extremely profitable use. On balance, in Vietnam the vulnerability to mines and the absence of major combat formations in prepared positions where the location is accessible lead me to the position that an infantry battalion will be more useful to you than a tank battalion at this stage.

B. I have seen few reports on the use of the light tanks available to the Vietnamese and draw the inference that commanders are not crying for their attachment for specific operations.

C. Distances and planned areas of employment of the 1st Division are such that the rapid movement of troops could be slowed to the rate of movement of the tanks.

D. The presence of tank formations tends to create a psychological atmosphere of conventional combat, as well as [recalling] the image of French tactics in the same area in 1953 and 1954.[11]

Furthermore, General Westmoreland in Saigon supported Johnson's position and expressed his own opposition to the deployment of the division's two mechanized battalions. Beside Johnson's reasons, Westmoreland added logistical considerations. The support and maintenance required by mechanized vehicles and tanks would, he argued, have broken the already shaky logistical services available. The experience of the 2nd Brigade, struggling for food and ammunition, was a clear warning in this direction. With Vietnam's small port capacity and a severely restrained US logistical presence, Westmoreland had to be extremely careful in introducing new forces. Johnson and Westmoreland carried the day, although Seaman was able to keep his self-propelled M110s on the argument that he needed the range of their 8-in howitzers to supplement his 105mm and 155mm guns.

Johnson's decision left an already strained 1st Infantry Division short-changed of four battalions – two tank and two mechanized infantry. The two mechanized infantry battalions – the 1st and 2nd, 28th Infantry Regiment – were then converted to infantry, while

Preparing to deploy. The task of deploying a whole combat division from the US to Vietnam was daunting, yet it was accomplished. Here a train-load of M113s from 1-4th Cavalry has been prepared for movement to the West Coast embarkation ports. (US Army)

Troops of the 1st Infantry Division preparing to board trains at Fort Riley, Kansas, to California. (US Army)

Landing at Vung Tau. The men of the 2nd Battalion, 16th Infantry Regiment, 'Rangers' are unloading from a US Navy Landing Craft on 12 July 1965. (US Army)

Beside M48 tanks, the squadron was also equipped with M114 scout vehicles. The M114 was a subpar vehicle, and operational tests conducted by the ARVN in South Vietnam had proven the vehicle unsuitable for off-road movement. Furthermore, even though the vehicle had been designed to be amphibious, Vietnamese crews had found it almost impossible to enter or exit waterways. A readily available alternative was the excellent M113 that had received plenty of praise from ARVN operators and had been successfully used in Vietnam from 1963 onward. Surplus M113s were also readily available at Fort Riley from the two converted mechanized infantry battalions. Yet even this change required considerable give and take between Seaman and his superiors.

the two tank battalions were replaced by two infantry battalions – the 1st and 2nd, 2nd Infantry Regiment – from the 5th Infantry Division. Non-deploying units, and the whole Fifth Army based in the United States, were combed for replacements, so that by the end of August, 170 officers and 2,900 enlisted men had been added to the division, bringing it up to 97 percent strength on the eve of deployment. This process was temporarily further complicated by another Pentagon official's meddling. Deputy Assistant Chief of Staff for Force Development, General Arthur L. West, submitted to General Johnson a report from a group he chaired on Vietnam's organisational and equipment requirements. This report suggested reconfiguring the 1st Infantry Division as a light infantry division, either in the States before deployment or in Vietnam. Alternatively, the report suggested the division delete items deemed not necessary for the mission, mainly vehicles, before deployment. Fortunately for the Big Red One, Johnson felt that "changing horses completely at this stage could cause serious turbulence within the division that I am not prepared to cause right now".[12]

Pentagon interference notwithstanding, General Seaman still had some last-minute issues to solve. First, the division, like its 2nd Brigade already in Vietnam, was still equipped with the M14 rifle. The newer M16s were in short supply, and none were immediately available to the 1st Division. The Big Red One thus went to Vietnam with the old, trusty and heavy M14 rather than the M16, thereby temporarily adding another item – 7.62mm rifle rounds and their magazines – to the supply chain. The 173rd Airborne Brigade, the only other US Army unit deployed near Saigon, had already received the M16 and its 5.56mm ammunition. Then there was the issue of the 1st Squadron, 4th Cavalry Regiment. Seaman had been able to persuade Johnson to keep the armored cavalry unit with the divisions and to deploy it to Vietnam with its vehicles, M48 tanks included, so as to test the utility of armour in theatre. Yet reports from Vietnam itself forced Seaman to re-examine his decision.

With force structure, Pentagon meddling and shortages solved in one way or another, the 1st Division left Fort Riley for Vietnam. The official deployment order was received on 2 September. Most of the personnel moved by rail or air to West Coast harbours. The bulk of the division, including all the men, left Oakland on 12 ships between 16 September and 9 October 1965. Eight other ships carried additional materiel and left from the West Coast and even from Boston in the east. The little armada reached Vietnam between 1 and 30 October. Deployment to their base camps near Saigon was another huge undertaking, requiring escorted convoy and clearing operations, which were made by the 173rd Airborne Brigade and the 1st Division's 2nd Brigade. By early November, the whole division was ready for combat. Its 1st Brigade was ensconced near Phuoc Vinh, the 2nd Brigade remained at Bien Hoa and the 3rd Brigade settled at Lai Khe. Division headquarters was established at Di An, halfway between Saigon and Bien Hoa, and the divisional artillery and support deployed at Phu Loi, where the ARVN 5th Division was also based. With the division safely deployed, MACV decided to subordinate all US forces in the Saigon area to it. For a while, General Seaman was in charge of a super-division, but when the 25th Infantry started to deploy, a superior command was created, II Field Force Vietnam, and Seaman took its helm. The Big Red One also received a new commander, General William E. DePuy.

The man who had taken the Big Red One to Vietnam, and who would oversee it from the II FFV, was an artilleryman by trade. Seaman had been commissioned as a second lieutenant of artillery in 1934. He served as a military aide at the White House from 1935–38 and was then an instructor at West Point. He commanded an artillery battalion during the Second World War and after the war remained on active duty. Deployment to Vietnam with the 1st Infantry Division was his first combat engagement since 1945.

The man who replaced him is permanently linked to the Vietnam War. William Eugene DePuy entered the army in 1942 through a reserve commission in the infantry. In 1942 he was assigned to the

More and more men of the Big Red One landing on Vung Tau's beach from landing craft. (US Army)

90th Infantry Division, the same division where General Westmoreland spent the bulk of his Second World War service. He stayed with the division for the entire war and received a battlefield promotion to major in August 1944 and command of an infantry battalion. He held that position from Normandy until the Battle of the Bulge. During that period, he received one Distinguished Service Cross and three Silver Stars. In January 1945, he was promoted to lieutenant colonel and spent the closing months of the war serving in staff and operations roles in the division. After the war, he remained in the Army. In the period between 1945 and the outbreak of the Korean War, he attended the Command and Staff College and the Defense Language Institute. He also served as Acting Army Attaché in Budapest, where an incident left him with a broken leg. The Korean War broke out while he was recovering from that in the Walter Reed Hospital, Washington DC, and when his leg allowed, he was assigned to work on a new 'active' unit being created by the CIA under the command of Colonel Richard K. Stillwell. In this capacity he worked on clandestine operations and also had a brief stint working with the CIA in Asia. For a while he was director of operations in China. After two years with the CIA, he returned to the US Army. He was closely involved with its reorganisation after the Korean War and the Pentomic division concept.

In 1964, DePuy arrived in Vietnam to serve as Chief of Staff for Operations at MACV. At the time, General Harkins was still COMUSMACV and Westmoreland his deputy. The insurgency was being waged, but the main focus of the US mission was still mainly upon picking up the pieces of the broken RVN government after the generals' coup. In his position, DePuy saw the war intensify until by the end of 1964, the situation became militarily untenable. During this period, he was not only deeply involved in observing and analysing day-to-day Vietnamese operations but had an influential role in shaping MACV contingency plans for the commitment of US ground troops. This period helped him to shape his own concept of operations. When he replaced General Seaman at the helm of the 1st Infantry Division in March 1966, DePuy had a clear idea of what he wanted to accomplish. He wanted to remove the enemy main forces from populated areas and keep them off balance, but to do it in a way that emphasised American firepower rather than manpower. He was also focused on having battalions, as opposed to companies, in the field. In that he was in apparent disconnection with the COIN theorists arguing for the use of small units. But DePuy maintained that battalions were the smallest tactical unit with a sufficient command nucleus to manage an engagement and maintained that companies were too small and fragile for isolated operations.[13]

DePuy "had concluded that the trick to jungle fighting was to find the enemy with the fewest possible men and destroy him with the maximum amount of firepower".[14] This approach was evident in the 1st Infantry Division's operations from April onward. They were aggressive, depended on massive firepower and tried to entice the enemy to engage in set-piece confrontations. One element is critical here. For all his apparent focus on 'large battles', DePuy's operations were designed to remove enemy forces from the populated areas in the most cost-effective way, in time and manpower. Protecting the population centres from marauding PLAF and PAVN divisions was DePuy's objective.

25th Infantry Division, 'Tropic Lightning'

The last formation to arrive in time for ATTLEBORO, and to have an active role in it, was the 25th Infantry Division, known as the 'Tropic Lightning Division'. Stationed at Schofield Barracks on Oahu, Hawaii, after its redeployment from Korea, the 25th Division was the strategic reserve of both US Army Pacific and the whole Pacific Command (PACOM). It was also the command's own contingency unit. In this role it had not only figured prominently in all plans to reinforce Vietnam but had also spent considerable time in perfecting US Army COIN tactics and training to employ them in the field. It was not an exaggeration to say that under General Frederick C. Weyand, the division was the most prepared of the units to be sent to Vietnam.

In its garrison paradise, the 25th Infantry Division had one tank (2-34th Armor), one mechanized infantry (1-5th Infantry) and eight infantry battalions (4-9th Infantry, 1- and 2-14th Infantry, 4-23rd Infantry, 1- and 2-27th Infantry and 1- and 2-34th Infantry). The division had one cavalry squadron (4-4th Cavalry), three 105mm battalions (1-8th, 2-9th and 7-11th Artillery) and one combined 155mm/8-in battalion (3-13th Artillery). Aerial support was provided by the 25th Aviation Battalion. The 25th Infantry Division had provided volunteer door gunners to Vietnam from 1963 onward and had also participated in the contingency deployments to Thailand during the Laotian crisis in 1961–62. While its deployment to Vietnam seemed natural, PACOM had been reluctant to let the division leave Hawaii until a replacement reserve formation could be raised. Yet the division had kept abreast of the development. The excellent Jungle and Guerrilla Warfare Center administered by the division had also

One of the big 8" (203mm) M110 self-propelled howitzers General Seaman fought to keep with the division. Based on the same chassis of the 175mm M107, the M110 sacrificed the range of the M107 for greater accuracy and weight of shell. (US Army)

provided jungle training to a contingent of 1st Infantry Division soldiers before the latter formation departed for Vietnam.

Yet the increased escalation in South East Asia meant that the division had to deploy sooner than PACOM would have wished; certainly sooner than a suitable replacement as strategic reserve could be raised. Westmoreland counted on the division from July 1965, and the division itself was ready for the move. Orders to deploy one brigade to Vietnam arrived in the autumn of 1965. The 3rd Brigade, 25th Infantry Division – with the 1-69 Armor, 1-14th, 1- and 2-35th Infantry and 2-9th Artillery – was the first brigade to deploy. Movement to Vietnam was conducted smoothly and the brigade deployed to the II CTZ in December, replacing the 1st Cavalry Division in the Pleiku area. The rest of the division followed soon after. The 2nd Brigade arrived in January 1966 and was deployed north of Saigon, at Chu Chi. Division command followed in March, and finally the 1st Brigade arrived in April, both also deploying at Chu Chi. Later in 1966, when the 4th Infantry Division deployed to Vietnam, its 3rd Brigade was sent to Chu Chi to replace the 25th Division's 3rd Brigade and came under the operational control of the 25th Division, while the 4th Infantry Division took over the 3rd Brigade of the 25th. Effectively, the two 3rd Brigades were swapped between the divisions. The deployment of the 3rd Brigade, 4th Infantry Division was completed in September 1966, just in time for it to take part in Operation ATTLEBORO. The brigade also included an armor battalion, the 2-34th Armor, thus giving General Weyand some tanks back. The two 3rd Brigades were officially assigned to their controlling divisions in August 1967.

The movement of the 25th Infantry Division to Vietnam did not see the turbulence and interference that marked the 1st Infantry Division's deployment. One brigade after the other was put through pre-deployment exercises at the Division Jungle and Guerrilla Warfare Center. Weyand used the 2-14th Infantry, one of the last to deploy, to fill deploying battalions. Replacements were then used to fill the battalion so it was at full strength by the time of its deployment. Additionally, two full strength battalions from Alaska, the 4-9th and 4-23rd, were assigned to the division to avoid cannibalising other units. Not only did General Weyand resist attempts to remove his tanks, but he had both the 1-69th Armor and 3-4th Cavalry shipped to Okinawa, where their vehicles were refitted and updated. He was also able to replace M114s with modified M113s. The poor reputation of the former was known by the whole US Army. When his tank battalion deployed in Pleiku, Weyand requested a replacement. He obtained the 2-34th Armor, which deployed in September 1966 with the brigade from the 4th Infantry Division. The 25th Division had considered mechanized units an integral part of its COIN training and procedures, and Weyand vehemently opposed any idea of removing them from his order of battle.

Once in Vietnam, the 25th Division was almost immediately in combat. Its selected base area, Chu Chi, was a known enemy staging area. Underground storages connected by a tunnel system had been constructed in the area. While they were not the giant underground fortresses depicted in some accounts and in latter-day local museums, they were certainly a nuisance. US troops had to clear both the surface and the underground area before the Chu Chi base was fully operational, and constant minor incidents continued for weeks after the initial clearing operations.

Frederick C. Weyand was another artillerist like MACV's commanding general, Westmoreland. A Californian and Reserve Officers' Training Corps graduate from Berkley, Weyand had been assigned to active duty in 1940 with the 6th Artillery. He spent the majority of the early years of the Second World War in intelligence roles but gained Asian experience with his assignment as Assistant Chief of Staff for Intelligence to the CBI, the China-Burma-India command, in 1944–45. After the war, he served with the Military Intelligence Service, and from 1946–49 he was the Chief of Staff, Intelligence, for United States Army Forces, Middle Pacific, the forerunner of ARPAC, the name-change happening during Weyand's tenure. Then his career changed.

In 1949, leaving ARPAC intelligence, he attended the Infantry School at Fort Benning, graduating in time for the Korean War. He served in Korea as commanding officer, 1-7th Infantry Battalion, and Assistant Chief of Staff, G-3, of the 3rd Infantry Division in 1950–51, including during the Chosin campaign. Then he moved back to the US for further staff positions. He attended the Army War College in 1957–58. After that came another year of battalion command and more staff assignments until he was assigned to the 25th Infantry Division as Commanding General in 1964. He helped prepare the division for its contingency roles, namely a deployment to Vietnam.

General Weyand was not afraid of slugging directly with enemy main force units, but he saw conventional force-on-force battles – to use a 21st century definition – only as part of a larger design. He maintained that he was facing a complex environment where "no single element of the enemy's organization … if attacked alone, would cause the collapse of his force structure or the reduction of his will to resist".[15] For him, hunting main force regiments was productive only in so much as it allowed his forces to then apply pressure on the rest of the Viet Cong apparatus that directly affected the local people. Weyand's approach can be characterised more as 'clear and secure' than 'search and destroy'. In this he was helped by the fact he had kept his tanks and mechanized elements, allowing for quick, firepower-heavy reaction forces to be employed if needed, as well as by the intensive training the 25th Division had undergone before deployment, an RVN government presence that benefitted from 1964 efforts to improve its effectiveness, and, last but not least, by a relatively anaemic main force threat in his main area of operations, Hau Nghia Province, in the form of a single regiment, the 165th PLAF. Yet the 25th Infantry could not just concentrate itself on Hau Nghia, for as part of the II FFV the division had to be able to respond to threats throughout the III CTZ.

General William E. Depuy, the man who ended up defining the key operational concepts adopted by the US Army in Vietnam. An infantry officer by trade with combat experience in France and Germany, he was MACV operations officer in 1965 and then took the helm of the 1st Infantry Division from General Seaman in 1966. Westmoreland put him in command of Operation ATTLEBORO after the initial clashes between the 196th Infantry Brigade and the enemy. (US Army)

Adapting the US Army to Vietnam

With divisions and brigades training and deploying, the US Army was also adapting to the new theatre of war. Contrary to the image of an inflexible organisation, the US Army constantly adapted its tactics, weapons and organisation to improve performance in the field. Some adaptations were made in the field by the initiative of local commanders, while others were decided back in the United States. The majority of them concerned infantry battalions, but other units and branches were not forgotten.

A quick look at the battalion organisation shows that it was set up to be able to operate and survive in high-intensity threat areas and to deploy considerable organic firepower in the form of recoilless rifles and mortars. The battalion was organised to be able to fight both in Central Europe – against a heavily mechanized Soviet Army – and in peripheral theatres. It is also clear that battalions were expected to fight while outnumbered and against tank-supported thrusts. The lessons of Task Force Smith at Osan, Korea, in July 1950 had not been forgotten. Unlike the PAVN or PLAF battalions, that had been designed as a pure infantry force, destined to fight against other infantry, the US Army's battalions were, doctrinally and organisationally, designed to tackle a full spectrum of threats. The downside of this was that in a situation like Vietnam, the enemy did not employ armour in large numbers and consequently part of the battalion was relatively useless.

This in turn led to several adaptations in the field, often varying from division to division, if not from battalion to battalion. An obvious target for reorganisation, if not outright deletion, were the numerous 106mm RCLs. While these large recoilless rifles were indeed deployed to Vietnam, and in several case found use as long-range anti-sniper weapons, the majority of the time they were deployed in fixed emplacements in permanent or semi-permanent bases. They were rarely (if ever) taken into the field, and their crews were used to augment infantry platoons or simply make-good losses in them. There was a similar picture with the 4.2-in mortars, which were left in battalion firebases to augment deployed artillery but quickly ceased to be part of battalions in the field. They were heavy and their range was limited when compared to 105mm howitzers. With operations almost always conducted under the cover of artillery, the 4.2-in mortar become a superfluous weapon. The same could be said of the 81mm mortar. Again, the availability of plentiful artillery and air support, coupled with the weight of the weapon itself and its ammunition, made it redundant. More often than not, companies deployed in the field with only one mortar tube. On the other hand, while never mentioned in many accounts, the M67 RCL continued to be carried in the field by some units due to its usefulness as a bunker-busting weapon. The final item that did not find full use in Vietnam was the counter-battery radar. Despite the obvious need for counter-battery fire, the technical limitations of the equipment – coupled with the nature of the ground, which was often hilly or wooded – made the

Major General Frederick C. Weyand (1916-2010) the commanding officer of the 25th Infantry Division. Here together with Maj. Gen. K MacKay of the Royal Australian Army, commanding officer Australian Forces Vietnam, in a picture taken at Chu Chi in September 1966. (US Army/25th Infantry association)

The routine work of the US Army in Vietnam. Soldiers from the 2nd Battalion, 14th Infantry Regiment (Golden Dragons) are destroying a rice cache discovered during a routine patrol near Chu Chi. May 1966. (US Army)

available counter-battery radars unsuitable for field operations. While on paper they appeared an important addition and well-positioned to counter the importance of mortars in communist units, they appear to have been regarded largely as unreliable gadgets rather than effective instruments. They remained in use in large installations but were never completely successful in their intended role.

Adaptations were not limited to equipment; battalions also adjusted their organisation to the nature of the war and of the operations conducted. The usual situation saw two companies in the field while one was kept at the battalion's temporary base to protect attached artillery and provide a reserve. This in turn led to a sharp decrease in the actual combat strength of each deployed battalion. To offset this reduction, battalions often organised a fourth infantry company. With the bulk of deletions coming from the HHC or heavy weapons platoons, the HHC was reorganised, reducing its manpower and limiting it to administration and logistics functions. Excess personnel were then organised in the fourth line company. Likewise, the reduced complement of organic support weapons was grouped in 'Combat Support Companies', often with just four mortars – often 81mm mortars discarded by the infantry companies – and four RCL, and used for base defences. In this way, three companies, albeit smaller than a paper strength one, could be deployed for operations while a fourth one was available for defensive duty at the battalion base.

A similar process was applied to infantry platoons, with weapons squads often disbanded, allocating the M60 machine guns directly to infantry squads. The vagaries of casualties, reassignments, rotations and replacements often meant that platoons were operating under strength and with ad hoc organisations, rather than following their official Table of Organisation & Equipment (TO&E). It was not uncommon to see platoons with just two squads, often centred around their M60, rather than three.

All these adaptations were monitored by divisions, Field Forces and MACV. Lessons from the field were analysed and discussed, and – despite the image of an inflexible organisation – the US Army made a sincere effort to improve its combat effectiveness in Vietnam. In 1967, a new modified TO&E was authorised for battalions in Vietnam. This made the four infantry company approach official and reduced the scale of support weapons. The 1967 MACOV report endorsed and developed mounted infantry assaults.[16] It is worth noting that the trend of the US Army was in contrast to that of its opponent. They eschewed heavier weapons at lower organisational level, preferring instead to rely on their excellent artillery, armour and air support. It was not a reflection of 'cowardice', as hinted by North Vietnamese sources, but a reflection of technical superiority in the field. Artillery had its limitations, but on balance, relying on artillery was a much more cost-effective approach than depending on a plethora of heavier weapons in line companies. The latter hampered movement and complicated resupply.

Airpower

Beside artillery and helicopter gunships, US troops could count on additional support in the form of USAF and US Navy aircraft. While the importance of airpower had often been overstated, the use of air strikes – either in direct support of engaged troops or for operational purposes – was widespread and reasonably effective. Contrary to possible expectations, there were no dedicated close air support units at this stage of the war. Sorties were generated and allocated by centralised command centres based on ground units' requests, availability and priorities. It was a complex system, which was not helped at this stage of the war by multiple command and control authorities being involved in the process. Due to decisions in Washington and there also being plenty of inter-service rivalries, political sensibilities and almost feudal tendencies by the Commander in Chief Pacific, Admiral Ulysses Grant Sharp, and Ambassador William H. Sullivan in Vientiane, airpower was shared by no less than four commands.

Admiral Sharp in Honolulu was jealously overseeing raids over North Vietnam but had to cope with constant intervention from the White House and the Office of the Secretary of Defense. Sharp's planning also involved 7th Air Force Headquarters in Saigon if aircraft were taking off from South Vietnam. In turn, 7th Air Force in Saigon controlled air operations over South Vietnam, with some exceptions. It had direct authority only over USAF aircraft, and then only if their mission was restricted to South Vietnam. If they bombed targets in the North, control passed to PACOM. In addition, the 7th Air Force had no direct control of US Navy and USMC aircraft, the latter usually managed either by the 7th Fleet or the III MAF. Aircraft based in Thailand were controlled by a Thailand-based command to avoid giving the impression that Thailand was in some way subordinated to Vietnam. Of course, if these aircraft were bombing targets in South Vietnam they were then passed over to 7th Air Force. If their targets were in North Vietnam, PACOM or the 7th Fleet were involved. Finally, Ambassador Sullivan, through his military attaché

Airpower, here a Martin B-57B flying over Vietnam. The B-57 was a license produced variant of the British Canberra light bomber. It was used either in interdiction or close air support. (Albert Grandolini)

had control over missions bombing Laotian targets. Then there was the 13th Air Force at Andersen Air Base, Guam, which controlled the B-52s based there and used, by this stage of the war, in tactical Operation ARC LIGHT strikes. When bombing targets in South Vietnam, the B-52 sorties were requested by 7th Air Force and then dispatched by the 13th Air Force.

Despite its complication, the system, almost miraculously, provided effective control over South Vietnamese airspace. With no air superiority or air defence campaign to be conducted there, the system did not require extremely fast actions. Furthermore, 7th Air Force, being the MACV aviation component, also had US Navy and USMC officers, ensuring cooperation and coordination with these services. The 7th Air Force also had the authority to redirect flights for tactical emergencies, ensuring support could be provided extremely quickly when needed. Regional air control centres decentralised actual mission control.

Most of the strike missions inside South Vietnam were flown by F-100 Super Sabres. While an already aging design, the Super Sabre was effective and could carry a reasonable load along with its two internal 20mm cannons. Designed in the early 1950s as a supersonic replacement for the F-86 Sabre, the Super Sabre, or 'Hun', entered service in 1954. F-100 units were deployed to Vietnam or Thailand between 1962 and 1964 for temporary detached duty to provide CAS to ARVN units in South Vietnam and, from 1964 onward, interdiction strikes in Laos. With the expansion of American commitment in South East Asia, temporary duty was replaced by permanent basing. Ultimately, three F-100 wings would serve in the theatre. By 1965, the most common version used in Vietnam was the F-100D. After being sent north in the first strikes against North Vietnam, the F-100s were deemed too vulnerable for strike missions there after losses on 4 April 1965 over Than Hoa. Except for the specialised F-100F Wild Weasels, they would thereafter be used mainly in South Vietnam and Laos.

The other mainstay of tactical missions in South Vietnam was the almost mythical A-1 Skyraider, in its E and H versions. Flown by USAF, US Navy and Vietnamese Air Force (VNAF) units, the old Korean War veteran provided effective and reliable CAS. Even older than the F-100, its design dating back to the waning days of the Second World War in the Pacific, the Skyraider – affectionately known as the 'Sandy' or 'Spad' – was a propeller-driven aircraft with a remarkable load capacity. With an empty weight of 5,429kg, it had a load capacity of 3,600kg of ordnance in the A-1H version. Being propeller-driven, it enjoyed greater loitering time, while its slower speed increased accuracy, making it an appreciated support platform. The trade-off was increased vulnerability to ground fire. It was also one of the few aircraft to be shared by both the US Navy and Air Force (the others being the F-4 Phantom and A-7 Corsair II) before the F-35. The USAF interest in the A-1 was also a product of the Vietnamese conflict. The USAF evaluated the A-1 (based on the Navy AD-5 version at the time) during 1962 and 1963 for potential use in Vietnam. The objective was to "evaluate the A-1E Skyraider for possible use in counterinsurgency warfare, and gauge its maintenance supportability and requirements".[17] The tests were successful and the USAF A-1E version was produced by modification of existing Navy AD-5 variants. The first aircraft were deployed to Vietnam in 1963. US Navy A-1H/Js (designated AD-6 until 1962) were being transferred to the VNAF from 1960. As a side note, the first USAF A-1E Skyraiders sent to Vietnam operated with VNAF insignia and mixed crews: US pilots and VNAF observers. The USAF would acquire A-1Hs from Navy surplus from 1967 onward, in a rare case of the Air Force getting Navy hand-me-downs.

At the time of ATTLEBORO, both the Skyraider and Super Sabre were able to provide effective close air support and interdiction strikes using an ample panoply of air-dropped ordnance, from rockets to iron bombs, cluster bombs and napalm canisters. The Skyraider was able to carry all available ordnance, from 2,000lb bombs downward, making it a veritable 'bomb wagon'. Beside armed aircraft, a critical component of combat missions was the Forward Air Controller (FAC). Flying slow and light Cessna O-1 Bird Dog aircraft, the role of the FAC was to act as a link between the ground controller and the strike aircraft. They were supposed to mark targets with smoke rounds, direct the fighter-bombers' passes and also act as a communication relay due to the heavy forested terrain.

With the air defence threat in the III Corps area comprising only heavy machine guns and light cannons, Skryraiders, Super Sabres and Bird Dogs were not excessively vulnerable. The progressive introduction of heavier guns and finally missiles after 1971 would reduce the survivability of the Skyraiders, but in 1966 that was in the future. In 1965 and 1966, the main issue was not enemy fire but one of coordination. No one before, not even American forward observers, had really closely coordinated artillery, gunships and aircraft. What was known was that there were dangers in the too close employment of all three elements. USAF official doctrine had eschewed CAS missions for just that reason. Initial attempts highlighted issues, and at times, interruption of artillery fire to allow flyers to enter the battle area was counterproductive for the troops on the ground. Yet effective methods were developed, often involving boundary systems to employ all three elements in coordination on different segments of a battlefield. By October 1966, directing support was both an art and a science. While errors were always possible, ground observers and FACs had developed techniques allowing extremely effective and close fire and air support to be delivered on targets. Subsequently, the combination of artillery, air and helicopter support often sealed the fate of PLAF and PAVN units.

On a literal different level were the Boeing B-52D and F Stratofortress variants used for *Arc Light* missions. Jealously controlled by Strategic Air Command (SAC) HQ in Omaha and only 'lent' to other commands, the huge nuclear-capable bombers were used for tactical missions in South Vietnam for a variety of reasons. Paramount was SAC's reluctance to risk aircraft from its nuclear deterrent force to surface-to-air missile (SAM) fire and losses over North Vietnam. Not until President Richard Nixon specifically ordered the B-52s north in 1972 were the Stratofortresses employed in a strategic bombing role. There had been political reasons, the Johnson administration being careful in not giving the impression of an all-out war against Hanoi. B-52s were consequently used as tactical bombers in support of ground operations. Carrying more than 24 tons of bombs and flying at an altitude that made them basically invisible and silent, cells of three B-52s had the ability to flatten everything inside a 3km by 2km rectangle. The lengthy flying time from Kadena in Japan and then Guam, after the Japanese government pressured the USAF to avoid direct bombing missions from Okinawa, and complex control procedures made them an unwieldy weapon to employ on the battlefield. Targets had to be selected in advance, and missions required several hours of lead time. In several cases, enemy units had simply moved before the bombers even approached RVN airspace. On the other hand, when missions hit their intended targets, results were devastating. Even deep underground bunkers were vulnerable, and a single strike could virtually destroy an entire battalion.

The final and largely unsung component of the USAF effort was its transports. The Lockheed C-130 Hercules and Fairchild C-123 Provider assured strategic and operational mobility and sustainment. Thanks to their cargo capacity and the ability of both types to operate from relatively primitive airstrips, US Army battalions could be quickly moved by air close to the action (as would happen during ATTLEBORO). Even more importantly, large amounts of supplies could be provided to small airfields close to the scene of the action, ready to be delivered by helicopter flights. While the Vietnam War is usually associated with helicopter airmobility, the contribution made by USAF fixed-wing transport even to brigade operations could not be overestimated. Often, Hercules and Providers were at the centre of the supply hubs while Hueys and Chinooks were just the spokes.

Mike Forces

While ATTLEBORO was largely an American operation, local troops participated in it too. Actively involved were the troops of the III CTZ Mobile Strike Force: Mike Force for short. Mike Forces were semi-conventional forces trained and led by US Green Berets and comprising ethnic minorities from South Vietnam's border regions. They were an offshoot of the Civilian Irregular Defense Groups (CIDG) created by the US Special Forces (USSF) to patrol South Vietnam's borders and stem infiltration from Laos and Cambodia. By 1964, especially after the attack on the CIDG camp at Nam Dong in the I CTZ, it had become painfully evident that while reasonably successful, CIDG camps had become prime targets for regiment-size attacks, something with which they were not equipped to deal. Due to their remote location, ARVN relief forces were, more often than not, unable to reach them in time, if at all. In response, the 5th Special Forces Group had raised and trained assault companies to act as reaction forces. The rationale was that airlifting these units would have bolstered camp defences in time. By 1965, there was a battalion-equivalent per ARVN Corps Tactical Zone. In the III CTZ, detachment A-302 at Bien Hoa had raised the 3rd Mobile Strike Force Command (MSFC) with a strength oscillating between four and five companies. Recruits were largely Nung, ethnic Chinese, but with time, more and more Cambodians living on the two sides of the border were recruited.

Each Mike company comprised three infantry platoons organised like US ones, with three infantry squads of 11 men each plus a weapons squad, a weapons platoon and a small scout platoon. While on paper this organisation was along US lines, in practice the Mike companies lacked the heavier weapons found in their US Army counterparts. For example, the infantry platoon weapons squad was not always present. Equipment allocation was also different. M1/M2 carbines were the standard individual weapons, supplement by Second World War-vintage Browning automatic rifles, M1919A6 light machine guns, 3.5-in bazookas and 60mm mortars. The only concession to 'modern' equipment was the three M79 grenade launchers allocated to each company. While the troops were indigenous, the officers and NCOs were American. The company commander was a Special Forces officer, usually a 1st Lieutenant, as was his executive officer. The four platoon commanders were likewise USSF 1st Lieutenants or senior NCOs. Captains were used in other roles, often as CIDG camp CO. Usually, a USSF medic was assigned to each company, supervising the platoon medics who were-USSF trained locals.

4

PRELUDE: SU DOAN 9 AGAINST THE BIG RED ONE NORTH OF SAIGON

Vietnam was and is a land of contrasts, myths and stereotypes. Even its geography and orthography have been distorted in the popular imagination, often by the horde of movies filmed in Hawaii or the Philippines. What in 1965 and 1966 was called the III Corps Tactical Zone is a clear example. Bordered from the south by the Mekong Delta and from the north-east by the Central Highlands, in 1965 this area comprised 18 percent of the RVN's total landmass, 25 percent of its population, around 4 million people and its capital, the sprawling Saigon with the Cholon suburb. The land was neither covered in continuous rice paddies nor unending jungle. From Saigon to the Cambodian border, the lay of the land was relatively flat, dotted by gently rolling hills. Of course flat did not mean Ukrainian-style tank-friendly country. Vietnam is a land of vegetation, and the III CTZ was no exception. Being sandwiched by the delta marshlands and the Central Highlands also meant that features from these areas spilled into the III CTZ. Geologically speaking, this was the piedmont area of South Vietnam. It was bounded on the north by a small section of highlands, characterised by rugged, forest-covered hills. The eastern section was instead bounded by the south-east coastal lowlands, characterised by sandy beaches, wide, flat-floored valleys and rice fields. A small section of the Mekong Delta was located within the southern boundary of the III CTZ. South of Saigon itself lay the Rung Sat Special Zone, a mangrove swamp covered in dense vegetation and crisscrossed by small waterways.

The soil is made of red clay, which tends to quickly turn into mud when wet. Even in the dry season, a sudden rain shower can turn the battlefield into a quagmire. Northward from Saigon city, and north-east from the Saigon River, the area was dotted with small rolling hills, woods, villages and giant rubber tree plantations, such as the famous Michelin Rubber Plantation. Vegetation could vary from brushes and tall grass to trees, but it was not the triple-canopy jungle so dear to filmmakers. The area was also crisscrossed by roads and paths, from large national highways such as the RC 13 to small tree cutters' tracks. Even the Michelin Plantation had its share of roads and paths. Most of these roads were unpaved, adding to the woes of the wet season.

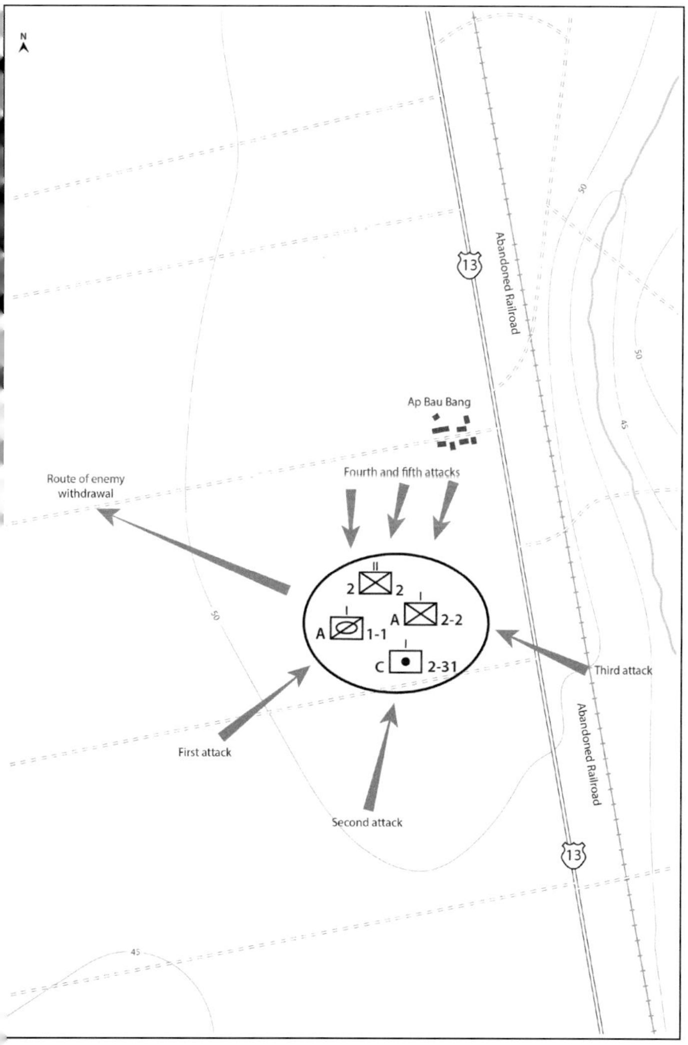

The battle of Ap Bau Bang, 12 November 1965. Elements of 9th PLAF Division attacked a US position manned by A Company, 2-2nd Infantry, A Troop, 1-4th Cav (without tanks), and C Battery, 2-31st Arty. (Map by George Anderson)

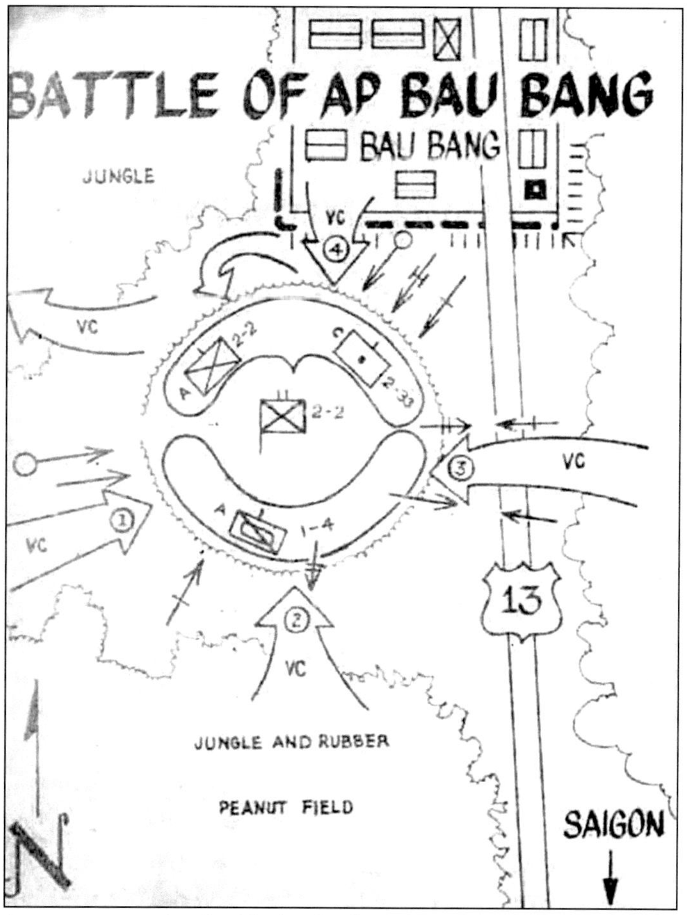

A contemporary sketch of the battle of Ap Bau Bang, the first clash between the Big Red One and the 9th PLAF Division. First the position was attacked by fire with mortars (1), then an infantry attack hit the cavalry positions (2), followed by another (3). The main attack was launched from the north (4) supported by heavy weapons located in the Ap Bau Bang Village. (US Army)

Like the rest of South Vietnam, the weather was dominated by the two seasonal monsoons. The south-western monsoon dominated the area from May to September, bringing with it rains and clouds, reducing vehicle mobility and flying time for aircraft and helicopters. From late September to late March was the dry season. This was when the north-eastern monsoons hit Vietnam, but they were stopped by the Annamite Mountains further north than the III CTZ, thus shielding the area from cloud and rain. The period from October to March was consequently ideal for offensive military operations for both sides.

From a military standpoint, the area was dominated by several key features for both sides, Saigon being the most obvious of them. Saigon's presence made the III CTZ a critical area for the two warring parties, capturing or defending it being a clear-cut geographical and political objective. Not only was Saigon an important political symbol, it was also the largest city of South Vietnam. It was served by an important harbour and possessed one of the largest airports in the country, Than Son Nhut, making it a critical supply hub for MACV. Besides Saigon and Than Son Nhut, critical facilities were the deep water port at Vung Tau and the military airbase at Bien Hoa. Vung Tau was one of the main entry points into Vietnam for American and allied troops. It was also an important logistical hub that MACV engineers were expanding. While administratively an independent province, for practical purposes it was connected to Phuoc Thuy Province, by 1966 the base of the 1st Australian Task Force. Bien Hoa, at least until 1965, came under attack from Viet Cong rocket and sapper assaults, which had taken a toll of VNAF and USAF aircraft stationed there; it was to protect that base that Westmoreland originally brought the 173rd Airborne Brigade from Okinawa. Until the commitment of the 1st and 25th Infantry Divisions, the only other regular troops in the areas were the 5th ARVN Infantry Division deployed north of Saigon and the 25th Infantry Division, a newer and less effective unit, to the west.

The Central Office for South Vietnam had three critical 'base areas', a collection of camps, logistical infrastructures, hospitals and training camps. To the north, close to the Cambodian border in Tay Ninh Province, there was War Zone C, which by 1965 was the home of the 9th PLAF Division. North-east of Saigon, in Long Khanh, War Zone D was the haunt of the 7th PAVN Division. Phuoc Thuy was the main staging area of the 5th PLAF Division. Between War Zones C and D there was the ambiguously defined Iron Triangle, a smaller base area connecting the two War Zones, so named because it was roughly shaped like a triangle. It was the arena where the 9th PLAF Division and the US 1st Infantry Division fought for supremacy for several months.

In 1967, units from the 25th Infantry Division recovered documents about the 9th PLAF Division. One of them, extolling the combat achievement of the division, stated that the 9th PLAF had never been defeated. Such a conclusion would have raised several eyebrows of the troops of the 25th Infantry Division and 1st Infantry Division.[1] The story of the 9th PLAF Division actually involved a long series of defeats against American and even South Vietnamese forces. By October 1966, the 9th PLAF Division had been bested in every encounter with American forces, propaganda notwithstanding.

While Operation ATTLEBORO was the first American combat action involving units from more than one division, it was not the first encounter between US and PLAF troops in the area north of Saigon. ATTLEBORO was just the latest round in a series of clashes between the 9th Division and its main American opponent, the 1st Infantry Division. In the period between November 1965 and October 1966, US units started to aggressively encroach in areas that Colonel Cam, the 9th PLAF commander, considered safe. Cam's soldiers tried to thwart American moves as much as possible. The year preceding ATTLEBORO was characterised by constant clashes between US forces and elements of the 9th Division, often of battalion or regiment strength. These battles set the stage for ATTLEBORO and also highlighted several key factors that would feature prominently throughout the operation, namely the inability of the 9th Division to perform its main mission and the steadily increasing gap between Colonel Cam's appreciation of events and the actual outcome of the fighting. This in turn influenced COSVN's decision to increase its conventional, large-scale efforts to achieve a decision in the 1966–67 dry seasons.

Round 1: Hill 65

The organisation of the 9th Division in late 1965 was a product of Hanoi's escalation of its war against the Republic of Vietnam. The division's main target was supposed to be the ARVN, but matters did not turn out that way. With Washington countering Hanoi's escalation and MACV's decision to interpose US troops between an apparently collapsing ARVN and the enemy, American forces had to be engaged. The 9th Division spent its time mainly fighting Americans troops, now deploying in the area north of Saigon in considerable strength. The first encounter took place on 8 November between the PLAF 3rd Battalion, 271st Regiment and the American 1-503rd Infantry, at the time assigned to the 173rd Airborne Brigade. The 173rd had launched Operation HUMP, a search and destroy operation in War Zone D north of Bien Hoa aimed at the 272nd and 274th Regiments, the latter part of the 5th PLAF Division. Lieutenant Colonel John Tyler's troopers were conducting company-sized patrols when C Company, commanded by Captain Henry Tucker, was attacked by the 3rd Battalion of the 271st. Firing from prepared positions and supported by plenty of machine guns, the PLAF soldiers pinned down C Company. To reduce the impact of American supporting arms, the Viet Cong tried to close with the Americans with a sudden attack, but they were stopped by determined infantry fire from C Company. With the Americans pinned and fixed in place, the 3rd Battalion tried a textbook flanking assault enveloping Tucker's right flank. The attack failed when it was hit in turn by the 1-503rd's B Company, advancing in support of C Company. Colonel Tyler had anticipated the 271st's movements and countered them, B Company hitting the flanking force in the rear. Undeterred, the 271st repeated the manoeuvre but was again stopped. Later, a third flanking manoeuvre was attempted on the same flank, hoping to envelop both B and C Companies. This third envelopment was foiled in turn by A Company, 1-503rd. While fighting continued, by mid-afternoon the 271st was forced to retreat. While a contested clash, the issue was never in doubt.

During the encounter, the 1-503rd suffered 49 KIA and 83 wounded, but the PLAF 3rd Battalion was severely mauled. The 271st's losses are unknown, but 173rd Airborne estimates put them at around 400.[2] The 271st Regiment had lured the US troops into a perfect ambush zone of its choosing and had fought in a way that reduced the impact of American artillery, but nevertheless it had failed. Despite claims to the contrary, US infantry had shown they were perfectly capable of grappling with the enemy and beating them back. The first round had gone straight to MACV and its airborne troops.

Round 2: Ap Bau Bang

Four days later, a mixed force from all the 9th PLAF Division's regiments attacked the 2-2nd Infantry, reinforced by Troop A, 1-4th Cavalry and Battery C, 2-33rd Artillery from the 1st Infantry Division under Lieutenant Colonel Shuffer. This was the first encounter in the long contest between the two divisions. The battle was the by-product of an ARVN redeployment. The commander of the ARVN 5th

Troopers from A Troop, 1-4th Cav watch a USAF airstrike by an F-100 Super Sabre on enemy mortar positions during the battle of Ap Bau Bang. (US Army)

Division, realising that enemy forces lurked north of Bien Hoa beyond Hill 65, wanted to reposition one of his regiments to counter them. He asked the US 1st Division to provide road security and clearance for the move. MACV readily complied and US troops duly secured the road, allowing for unmolested passage of the ARVN troopers. That mission accomplished, American forces from the 3rd Brigade of the 1st Infantry Division conducted a search for a suspected enemy concentration in the area of the Michelin Plantation. The operation was labelled BUSHMASTER I. The American movement sparked Cam's interest: assaulting one of the American units posted to guard the road was a perfect opportunity to 'kill the Americans'.

The encounter happened close to the hamlet of Ap Bau Bang in the early hours of 13 November. Colonel Shuffer had placed his units south of the hamlet in a night defensive position while waiting for further orders. It turned into a disaster, but not in the way Cam had predicted or hoped. Cam's battalions launched several uncoordinated attacks against the American defences. The first assault, starting at 0605 hours, was beaten back by a mounted counter-charge of a cavalry platoon on M113 ACAVs. The second attack was beaten back by infantry and vehicle fire, as was the third. The fourth attack, intended as Cam's main effort, hit the US perimeter from a different direction. Launched at 0700 hours and using the hamlet and a wooded area as cover, it was supported by intense mortar, recoilless rifle and machine gun fire. Although a sapper squad succeeded in destroying a 105mm howitzer from Battery C with a satchel charge, the issue was never in doubt. Infantry weapons, ACAV-mounted machine guns and beehive rounds from Battery C savaged the attackers. US Air Force A-1 Skyraiders were also on the scene just before 0700 hours, adding to the carnage. A fifth attack occurred at 0900 hours but met the same fate, this time a flight of F 100 fighter-bombers providing close air support for the US troops. By then Shuffer had also recalled the rest of his infantry battalion. At the start of the engagement, only A Company of 2-2nd was inside the perimeter. The entire affair was concluded by 1330

Beside F-100s, A-1 Skyraiders also played an important role at Ap Bau Bang. Here USAF A-1Es are in flight over Vietnam in 1965. (USAF)

A M101 from C Battery is firing over open sights on enemy forces during the battle. (US Army)

Casualties from the battle are treated by a member of the division's 1st Medical Battalion. After first aid the wounded would be moved by helicopters to the Division Hospital at Bien Hoa. (US Army)

hours. For the loss of 20 KIA and 103 wounded, the Americans killed 146 of their enemies. After-action reports estimated that another possible 50 bodies were removed by the enemy.

PLAF wounded and other losses were not reported, but considerable quantities of equipment were salvaged from the battlefield. Considering that Cam has attacked one infantry company, one cavalry troop and one artillery battery with at least four of his own battalions, plus two more in reserve, the results were meagre and communist casualties were indeed severe. Captured documents from the 273rd Regiment indicated 30 KIA and 58 wounded, the regiment providing only two companies for the actual attack, plus the two battalions in reserve. Yet Cam somehow considered the engagement a resounding victory. In his memoirs, he claimed he reported his success to the commander of the whole theatre, General Tran Van Tra. It was just the first of a series of unbelievable claims. During the following months, 9th Division's claims appeared ever-more removed from reality.

On the American side, it is worth noting the absence of the 1-4th Cavalry's M48 tanks. At this stage of the war, General Westmoreland was still sceptical about the employment of tanks in combat operations. Lewis Sorley claimed that MACV hostility toward tanks was a product of Westmoreland's ignorance of their use and general lack of knowledge.[3] As often is the case where Sorley is concerned, the attack on Westmoreland is both gratuitous and unwarranted. Westmoreland's reservations on the use of tanks (rather than armour in general) were more a by-product of terrain analysis and a perceived lack of usefulness, due to distorted reporting of French tank operations in the region.[4] In addition, maintenance and spares-intensive units like tank battalions would have stretched thin MACV supply establishment, one of the main constraints on the whole build-up in Vietnam. Furthermore scepticism on the usefulness of M48s in Vietnam was not limited to Westmoreland or his officers at MACV. As already discussed, the Army Chief of Staff, General Harold K. Johnson, was even more sceptical than Westmoreland. I

2nd Lt John Libs, C Company, 1-16th Infantry and his platoon command group survey the situation before advancing on enemy position in October 1965. They carry M14 rifles and M60 machine guns. (US Army)

An M48A1 Patton 90mm Gun Tank from 1-4th Cavalry, Quarterhorse, 1st Infantry Division in 1965-66. The design of the M48 was initiated in 1951 under the designation T-48: originally based on the M47, it featured a new turret and a redesigned hull, without the machine-gunner's position, reducing the crew to four. Nearly 12,000 M48s were manufactured from 1952 to 1959. Over 600 M48s were deployed with US forces in Vietnam, initially by the US Marines in 1965, mostly in battalions consisting of 57 tanks. This illustration shows an example typical of 1965-1966, void of any special modifications or markings. (Artwork by David Bocquelet)

An M48A3 Patton 90mm Gun Tank from 2-34th Armor, Dreadnaught, assigned to the 25th Infantry Division. Originally part of the 4th Infantry Division, the battalion was swapped with the 25th's own 1-69th Armor. The M48A3 could be distinguished by the new engine deck – covering a diesel engine as opposed to the gasoline one of the A1 variant – and by the riser under the M1 cupola providing better all-around vision. The tank is covered in stowage and the personal belongings of the crew, but lacks the usual modification seen in Vietnam: the removal of the .50 cal heavy machine gun and its repositioning above the M1 cupola. (Artwork by David Bocquelet)

An M107 175mm self-propelled gun from 8-6th Field Artillery, Centaurs, 1st Infantry Division, with battalion crest and shield shown inset. Introduced to service in the early 1960s, the M107 was the almost twin brother of the M110, which used the same chassis. With a range of 32,700 metres, the 175mm gun was the longest-ranged artillery piece the US Army employed in Vietnam – which was of crucial importance because of the long range of the Soviet-made M54, widely used by the North Vietnamese forces. Moreover, the M107 was lighter than the M53 155mm self-propelled gun it replaced, and thus air transportable. Its 13mm aluminium armour provided protection for the driver only, and was sufficient for defence from small arms fire and shell splinters. (Artwork by David Bocquelet)

The M113 was a fully tracked armoured personnel carrier (APC) developed by the Food Machinery and Chemical Corporation (FMC) to replace the older M59 of the US Army from 1961. First deployed to South Vietnam only a year later, it quickly became the most widely used armoured vehicle in the Vietnam War, and which proved capable of breaking through heavy thickets in the middle of the jungle, and attacking and overrunning enemy positions. This example was operated by the 2-22nd Infantry, Triple Deuce. It was a standard M113 APC without any modification, but is shown with the crew's personal gear and additional equipment attached to the top deck. (Artwork by David Bocquelet)

The 'track' shown here, nicknamed 'Alice's Restaurant' and 'To The Alps', was another standard M113 APC operated by the 2-22nd Infantry, Triple Deuce, the insignia of which is shown inset. Originally one of the infantry battalions of the 4th Infantry Division, the 2-22nd was instead assigned to the 25th Infantry Division by the time it participated in Operation ATTLEBORO. As usual by this time, the crews of this unit frequently deployed it to clear the way through heavy bush, while the infantry followed on foot immediately behind. (Artwork by David Bocquelet)

The opportunity to test the 'mechanized' infantry concept, and the versatility of the M113 spawned a wide variety of adaptations, mostly aimed to enable them to run 'reconnaissance in force', and 'search and destroy' operations. This example was operated by the 1-4th Cavalry, Quarterhorse (insignia shown inset). Notable is the shield protecting the commander and his .50 cal machine gun mounted on the cupola: this modification was introduced by ARVN officers and US advisors after the battle of Ap Bac in 1963. Two lighter M60 machine guns were mounted, one on each side of the hull, with additional shields for their gunners. This modification was also adopted by other US Army units deploying to Vietnam. (Artwork by David Bocquelet)

The US Department of Defense originally acquired 3,200 Cessna L-19s between 1950 and 1959 and distributed them to the US Army and the US Marine Corps for artillery spotting, frontline-communications, medevac and training. By the time of the Vietnam War, the designation of the type had been changed to O-1 Bird Dog, and it was introduced to service by the US Air Force as a Forward Air Controller (FAC) aircraft. This example – serial number (0)11924 – was assigned to the 19th Tactical Air Support Squadron, officially based at Bien Hoa, but often operating from other locations, supporting operations across the entire III CTZ. The Bird Dogs were unarmed except for white phosphorus rockets carried under the wing and used to designate targets. (Artwork by Tom Cooper)

The Martin B-57B Canberra was based on the design of the English Electric Canberra bomber of British origin. This example wore the serial number 53-3925 and was assigned to the 13th Bomb Squadron, 405th TFW, based at Tan Son Nhut or Bien Hoa between 1965 and early 1966. Notably it was still painted in silver-gray overall early during the Operation ATTLEBORO: later on it received the SEA camouflage pattern. The aircraft is shown carrying BLU-27 napalm tanks under the wings, and with two M117 demolition bombs underneath its bomb bay (usually, six of these were installed internally). When first deployed to Vietnam in 1964, the B-57Bs were used for reconnaissance, switching to strike missions in the South only in February 1965. The 405th TFW rotated crews from all its squadrons to Vietnam during its deployment there and the same aircraft could be flown by crews from different squadrons. (Artwork by Tom Cooper)

This illustration shows the Boeing B-52F-65-BW Stratofortress serial number 57-0144, nicknamed 'Mekong Express' that was operated by the 3960th Strategic Wing from Andersen AFB on Guam as of 1966. The 3960th SW was created in 1965 to control the growing force of B-52Ds and B-52Fs involved in ARC LIGHT missions over South Vietnam. This example is shown following the application of the South Bay modification, which enabled it to carry 24 750lb (354kg) M117 bombs on two multiple ejector racks under each wing – installed on the hardpoint intended for Hound Dog cruise missiles – and 27 such bombs inside the bomb bay. The aircraft is shown in its 'intermediate' colours: with silver-gray on top surfaces and sides, but with its white undersurfaces already re-painted in matt black. Subsequently, it received the SEA camouflage pattern. (Artwork by Tom Cooper)

As of 1965-1966, the North American F-100 Super Sabre was the most numerous tactical fighter-bomber of the US Air Force. Unsurprisingly, the type clocked the most combat sorties of all types during the Vietnam War. This F-100D-25-NA (serial number 55-3604) is shown during its service with the 416th Tactical Fighter Squadron, 'Silver Knights', which was a part of the 3rd Tactical fighter Wing, based at Bien Hoa AB as of 1966. At the time, it was still in natural metal overall, and wore the blue flashes of the squadron on the fin. The F-100D was armed with two 20mm cannons, the extensive use of which frequently left thick cordite marks down the front fuselage. External armament typically included a pair of Mk.82 or M117 bombs on the inboard underwing pylons and a pair of napalm tanks on the outboard pylons. (Artwork by Tom Cooper)

The Northrop F-5 Freedom Fighter came into being as a private venture of that company, the aim of which was to develop a lightweight, multi-role fighter-bomber. The US Air Force did not want it, but the Department of Defense began marketing it as an affordable solution for 'friendly Third World countries'. To bolster the confidence of potential customers, in 1965 the decision was taken to work-up a squadron with 16 jets for a deployment to Vietnam. Thus came into being the F-5C shown here, serial number 64-13317, assigned to the 4503rd Tactical Fighter Squadron (Provisional), based at Bien Hoa AB as of January 1966, by which time this unit was subordinated to the 3rd TFW. As combat testing advanced, the squadron became a regular unit in March of the same year. All of its F-5s were camouflaged in the SEA camouflage pattern. Standard armament consisted of pair each of Mk.82s and napalm tanks. (Artwork by Tom Cooper)

The original Bell Model 204 was developed in the early 1950s in reaction to a US Army requirement for a medevac and utility helicopter. First flown in 1956, it entered operational service as the UH-1 Iroquois, colloquially the 'Huey', but initially proved underpowered, leading to the development of the more powerful UH-1A, and then the UH-1B in 1960. While still unsatisfactory, suffering from aerodynamic deficiencies and lack of space for passengers, UH-1As and UH-1Bs were pressed into service with the 101st Airborne Division, and then converted into gunships through the installation of ground-attack armament. This UH-1B was operated during Operation ATTLEBORO by an unidentified unit. Still underpowered and loaded with a pair of M60 machine guns in the former troop compartment, and two M60 external armament sub-systems, the version often struggled to keep the pace with more advanced variants (see below). (Artwork by Luca Canossa)

The 'ultimate' UH-1B included an improved engine and a new rotor that enabled better manoeuvrability and a slight speed increase. However, constantly increasing requirement for additional firepower resulted in further upgrades of the UH-1B's weapons systems. Most of these were rather improvised by nature and included a wide range of combinations of rocket launchers, grenade launchers, and machine guns. UH-1s armed with rockets were commonly referred to as 'Frogs' or 'Hogs', while those carrying guns became known as 'Cobras' or, simply, 'Guns'. Experiences with improved enemy firepower led to the idea of installing anti-tank guided missiles, which could be deployed from long-range to knock out enemy heavy machine gun emplacements: the first such system was the French-made SS.11, illustrated on this example of an unknown US Army unit in 1966. (Artwork by Luca Canossa)

Further development of the Bell Model 204 resulted in the emergence of the Model 205, which included a more powerful engine, a bigger rotor, and a fuselage stretched by 104cm (41in), and entered operational service with the US Army in 1963, under the designation UH-1D. Deployed in Vietnam two years later, it saw widespread and intensive service as a troop transport. Called the 'slick', it usually had a pintle-mounted M60 machine gun installed on each side of the cabin. This example was operated by the 1st Aviation Battalion, 1st Infantry Division, one of the most important US Army units involved in Operation ATTLEBORO. By the time, all the UH-1s of the US Army were painted in matt forest green (FS34079) overall: nearly all Hueys of the 1st Infantry Division received white and red ID-strips down the boom during Operation ATTLEBORO. (Artwork by Luca Canossa)

The ultimate Huey variant of the Vietnam War became the UH-1H, itself a further improvement of the UH-1D. While visually next to indistinguishable from the earlier version, the UH-1H included self-sealing tanks and cockpit armour: it became the most-produced version, and over 7,000 were deployed during the Vietnam War. As clear from the unit insignia on the cockpit doors, and the white bear insignia applied on the boom, this example was operated by the 25th Aviation Battalion (organic to the 25th Infantry Division, headquartered at Chu Chi). This example is shown with its cabin doors completely removed, to enable easier embarkation and disembarkation for up to 13 passengers. (Artwork by Luca Canossa)

A PAVN soldier of the 101st Infantry Regiment, 7th Division. Part of the regular Army of the Democratic Republic of Vietnam, the soldier is equipped with a Soviet-produced SKS carbine (note the shape of the foldable bayonet). He is shown wearing standard equipment even if his uniform looks faded; PAVN troops could be issued green or khaki uniforms, but the dye tended to fade very quickly. When moving in relatively open areas, PAVN and PLAF troops often adopted camouflage to reduce the risk of being spotted by US Air Force or Vietnamese Air Force aircraft. Note the blanket roll used to carry rice while on the move. (Artwork by Anderson Subtil)

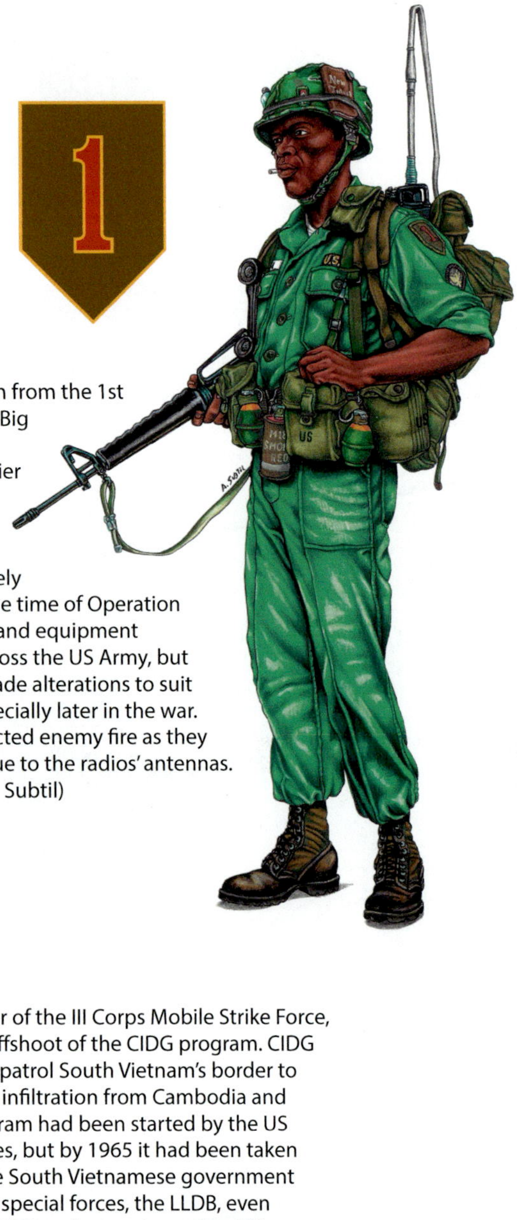

An American radioman from the 1st Infantry Division, 'The Big Red One', in 1966. The M16 rifle that the soldier is carrying was issued to the division in 1966, with infantry battalions being entirely equipped with it by the time of Operation ATTLEBORO. Uniform and equipment were standardised across the US Army, but soldiers in the field made alterations to suit the environment, especially later in the war. Radiomen often attracted enemy fire as they were easily spotted due to the radios' antennas. (Artwork by Anderson Subtil)

A South Vietnamese striker of the III Corps Mobile Strike Force, the Mike Forces – an offshoot of the CIDG program. CIDG troops were used to patrol South Vietnam's border to stem communist infiltration from Cambodia and Laos. The program had been started by the US Special Forces, but by 1965 it had been taken over by the South Vietnamese government and their special forces, the LLDB, even if the US SF involvement remained. The CIDG troops were recruited from ethnic minorities rather than the ethnic Vietnamese population. To back the chain of CIDG camps along the border, reaction forces – called Mobile Strike Forces – were formed, a battalion-equivalent per South Vietnamese Corps. The III Corps Mike Force was staffed largely by Nungs and headquartered at Bien Hoa. In 1966 Mike Force equipment was often non-standardised and the striker in the image has a mixture of different camouflage items in different tiger stripe patterns. Equipment was often of Second World War-vintage, in this case an M1 carbine with extended magazine. He is also carrying 7.62mm ammunition for the unit's light machine guns. The III Corps Mike unit wore red, white, and blue scarves. (Artwork by Anderson Subtil)

Two A-1H Skyraiders from the 1st Air Commando Squadron preparing for an attack run. The 1st ACS flew from Bien Hoa in 1965 before being moved to Pleiku in 1966, and then Thailand later in the war. (USAF)

A trio of F-100D Super Sabres over Vietnam. The photo was taken in 1965 and the aircraft are from the 481st Tactical Fighter Squadron "Crusaders", 33rd Tactical Group based at Tan Son Nhut. One of the Super Sabres already wears the South East Asia camouflage scheme, the other two are in natural metal. (USAF via Albert Grandolini).

A cold landing zone. Elements of the 1st Infantry Division making an air assault in a clearing. Some troops in the foreground are already moving out of the landing zone, while in the background UH-1D Hueys are still landing and taking off. (US Army)

An M113 of B Company, 2-22nd 'at rest', note the amount of stowage carried on its deck. (Mike Carpentier through 2-22 Infantry Association)

Despite all the supporting arms available to the US Army, locating the enemy was still the job of the infantry, often by drawing fire. Men of the 16th Infantry Regiment draw enemy sniper fire during an operation near Bien Hoa, 4 October 1965. (US Army)

Resupply in the field, a CH-47 delivers supplies to the 2-22nd during an operation. (Mike Carpentier through 2-22 Infantry Association)

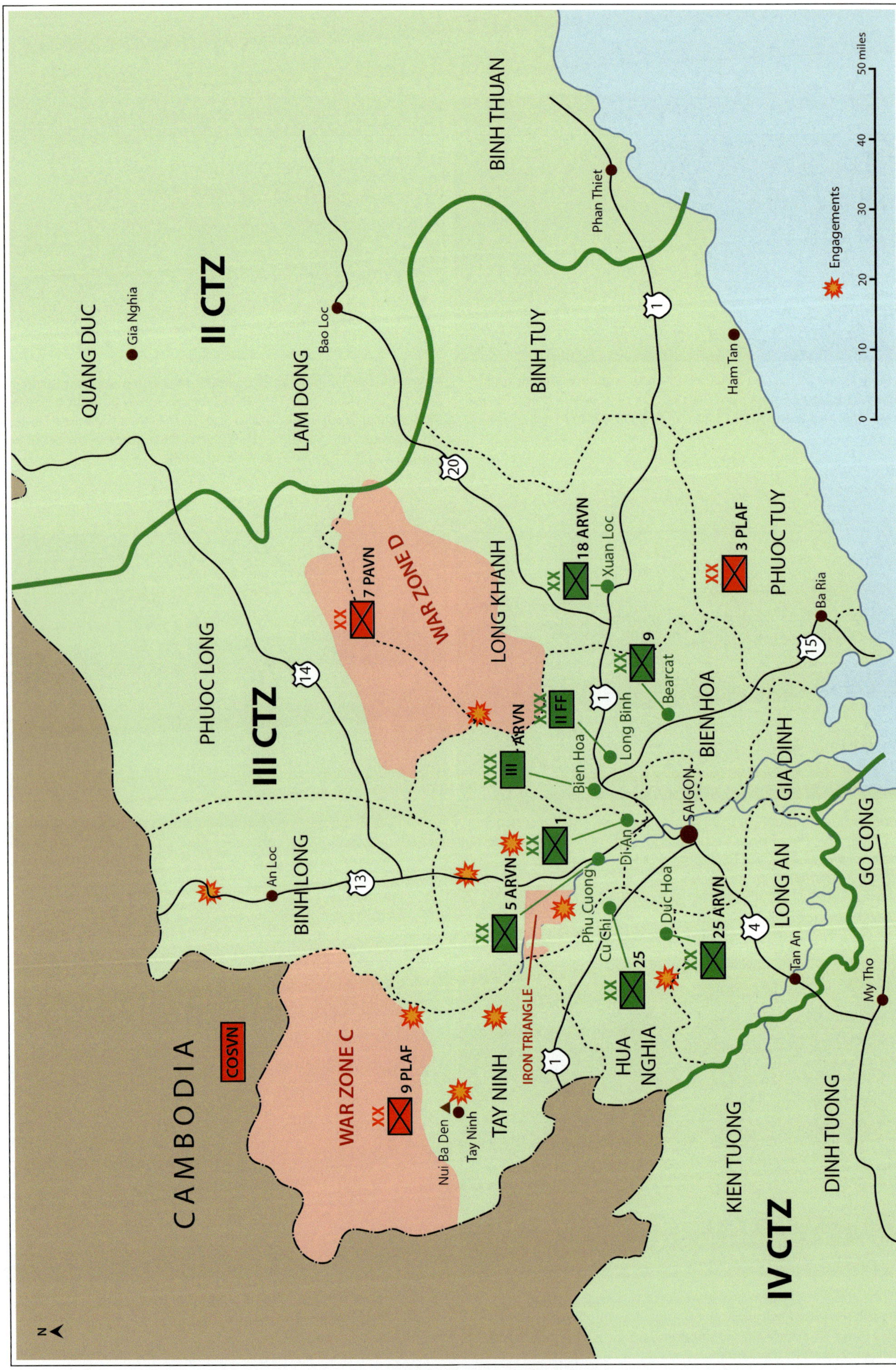

A map of the part of South Vietnam where Operation ATTLEBORO was run, in 1965-1966. (Map by George Anderson)

Small arms fire from Trung Loi village and machine gun fire from both sides of the road caused the lead platoons of C Company 2-28th Infantry to dismount vehicles and return fire. (US Army)

Just before the battle of Ap Nha Mat; a CH-47 is deploying a M101 105mm howitzer in the Michelin Plantation. (US Army)

was he who ordered General Seaman to drop his two tank battalions and consented to deploy the 1-4th's organic tanks only after strong dissent from Seaman.[5] Due to this general scepticism, A Troop had been directed to keep its Patton tanks in its base camp rather than taking them into the field. Proving the worth of the 90mm-armed Patton tanks would have to wait.

Round 3: Trung Loi

The 272nd PLAF Regiment brushed against the Big Red One again on 20 November, still as part of BUSHMASTER I. After having secured the movement of the ARVN troops from the 5th Division, General Seaman directed his 3rd Brigade, under Colonel Brodbeck, to enter the Michelin Plantation in force. Three battalions of infantry and one of artillery were involved, supported by heavy air strikes, including a B-52 *Arc Light* mission. The B-52 strike went as scheduled on 14 November, but the rest of BUSHMASTER I yielded meagre results. The operation was terminated by 20 November, with units returning to base. Several units moved by helicopter, but Lieutenant Colonel George S. Eyster's 2-28th Infantry was to move by road along Route 239 back to Lai Khe. The battalion was also escorting artillery from 2-33rd Artillery. Movement was made by trucks and M113 APCs borrowed from 1-4th Cavalry. Colonel Eyster's plan was to move by bounds, with one company and one battery establishing a firebase to cover each leap. Weather made Eyster's orderly move a nightmare. Route 239 was a quagmire and his convoy became a 3km-long column struggling forward at snail's pace no faster than 100 metres per hour.

Around 1820 hours, the head of the column, with two platoons of C Company under Lieutenant Colonel Frank R. Tims, was approaching the hamlet of Trung Loi. A sergeant from one of the lead platoons noticed an armed Viet Cong and opened fire. The enemy soldier was killed, but the column started to receive small arms fire from both sides of the road. They had walked into an ambush position set up by the 272nd along Route 239.

Colonel Tims ordered the two lead platoons to dismount and form a defensive perimeter. The platoons complied and engaged the enemy. In the meantime, the enemy was also engaging the middle of the column. C Company dismounted its mortar platoon, which immediately began firing on enemy positions. The mortars had to fire at maximum elevation to be able to hit targets just 20–30 metres from the sides of the road. The enemy in turn deployed a recoilless rifle to engage the mortars, but its crew and a replacement crew were quickly engaged and killed.[6] The attackers, later identified as the 4th Battalion of the 272nd Regiment, exploited a pause in American mortar fire, due to an ammunition shortage, to deploy a third crew to engage both the mortar platoon and C Company's command group. Mortar shells also started to pepper the column, while PLAF infantry closed to grenade range.

Despite the dire situation, the tide of the battle started to turn at that time. At 1840 hours, a flight of UH-1 gunships appeared overheard

The battle of Ap Nha Mat was a product of the 27 November 1965 attack on the ARVN 7th Regiment. This attack from the 9th PLAF Division brought Colonel Brodbeck's 3rd Brigade to the scene. Here soldiers of the 7th Regiment, ARVN 5th Division are shown patrolling. (US Army)

continued to receive small arms fire from the hamlet of Trung Loi. Permission was requested to direct supporting arms against the village. The South Vietnamese district chief was consulted and, with his consent, an air strike on the hamlet was authorised, after which enemy fire ceased. The whole column had cleared the ambush site by 2115 hours, with the infantry providing dismounted escorts for the vehicles, which were now carrying wounded. The force arrived at its destination, the village of Chon Than, at 2200 hours.

Six Americans had been killed in the ambush and 38 were wounded, six seriously. Six vehicles were badly damaged and could not be moved without assistance. Enemy losses were considerable. The actual body count was 70 KIA, with an estimated 100 wounded.[9] The 9th Division nevertheless reported a great success, with 100 Americans killed.[10] Yet BUSHMASTER had been a clear success for the 1st Infantry Division. It had not only inflicted serious losses on the 9th PLAF but had also accomplished the main goal of protecting the movement of the ARVN regiment. Considerable enemy supplies, including 81 tons of rice, had been captured in the area too.[11]

and began passes on the south-east side of the road, where the enemy appeared to be concentrated. The helicopters had to leave after 10 minutes but were replaced by a flight of USAF fighter-bombers that dropped napalm on the area. American air and helicopter support forced the 4th Battalion to leave their ambush positions and close on the road, where they were successfully engaged by C Company infantry fire.[7] American and ARVN artillery also started to rain accurate fire on the ambush positions. Support fire was conducted in close proximity of friendly positions, with the UH-1s strafing as close as 3 yards from the road, and napalm being dropped only 50 yards from C Company's positions.[8] By 1900 hours, C Company had weathered the worst of the ambush. An hour later, Tims and the troops started to move again, but

Round 4: Nha Mat

Trung Loi had not abated Colonel Cam's desire for decisive actions. He was still spoiling for a fight, and a fight is what he got in December. On 27 November, the PLAF's 271st and 273rd Regiments – the 272nd still licking its wounds – attacked the ARVN 7th Regiment near the Michelin Plantation. General Seaman concluded that the 7th had been

A soldier from a regular PLAF unit preparing to attack. The photo is staged but shows that regular PLAF units, as the 9th Division, were largely well-equipped. (Albert Grandolini).

A mortar crew from 2-2nd Infantry supporting ARVN troops during Operation BUSHMASTER II, just before Ap Nha Mat. (US Army)

literally shredded to pieces.[12] He reacted by ordering his 3rd Brigade, with two infantry and one artillery battalions, to move in to cover the South Vietnamese. Colonel Brodbeck's 3rd Brigade deployed with intelligence that the whole 9th PLAF Division and possibly even a VC local force battalion was concentrated south-east of the plantation. Brodbeck was ordered to give chase. Seaman provided him with a third infantry battalion so that Brodbeck could have one in reserve protecting the brigade HQ and two in the field. From 1–5 December, Brodbeck's battalions searched the area without any significant results. Then on 5 December, the 2-2nd Infantry – the victors of Bau Bang, still with Colonel Shuffer at the helm – found their prey.

Shuffer had launched a search of an area north of the hamlet of Nha Mat, approximately 8km from Bau Bang. B and C Companies were moving forward abreast, with the battalion HQ and A Company behind C Company. Around noon, Shuffer's men started to receive small arms, machine gun and mortar fire from bunkers and trenches to the front and from tree lines on the sides of the American line. The 2-2nd Infantry had stumbled on the 272nd's base

As usual, the enemy underestimated both the quality of US soldiers on the ground and their supporting fires. A 105mm howitzer from 3-33rd Artillery is providing support fire to the 2-2nd Infantry at Nha Mat. (US Army)

Hueys from 11th Aviation Battalion drop 2-2nd Infantry troops on the ground for a search and destroy mission. This insertion would lead to the battle of Ap Nha Mat. (US Army)

An official picture of Lieutenant Robert J. Hibbs (1943-1966), the hero of the second battle of Bau Bang (also called the battle of Lo Khe), and the first Medal of Honor recipient from the 1st Infantry Division in Vietnam. (US Army)

An M113 with ACAV kit from 1-4th Cav pictured in February 1966 at Tan Ninh, during an action by Big Red One against local forces. (US Army)

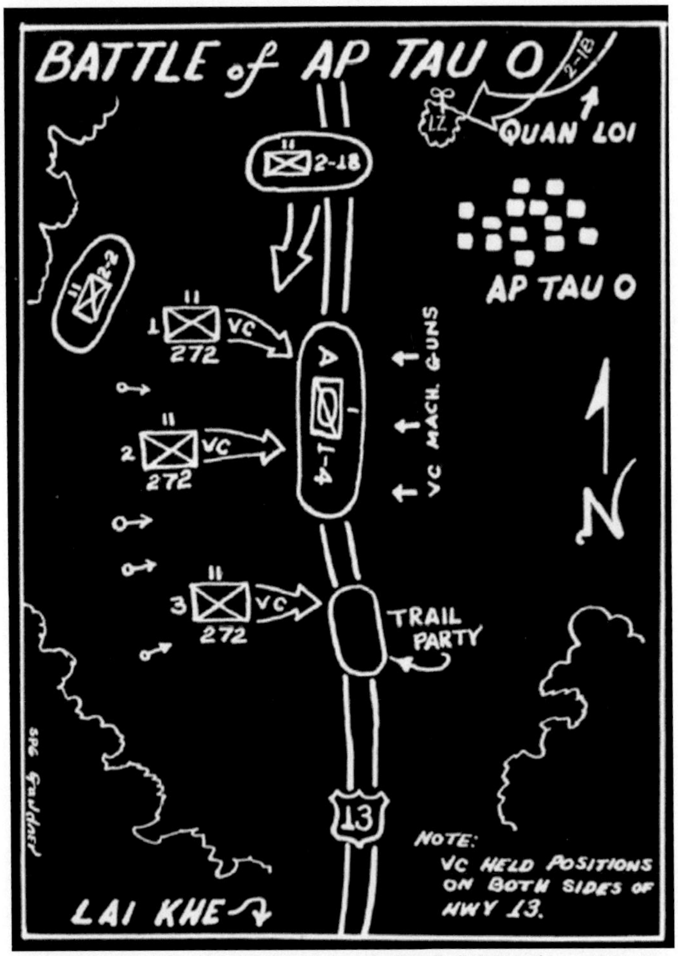

A contemporary sketch of the action at Ap Tau O. (US Army)

A 2-28th Infantry medic is treating a leg wound inside the battalion perimeter during the battle.

camp. How this happened is still a source of debate between the two sides. Colonel Cam asserted that his regiment had been rapidly redeployed to attack the American battalion, but Colonel Shuffer surmised that his battalion had hit the 272nd while it was recovering from its previous beatings. The fact that the 272nd was defending a prepared position rather than attacking and that, after the engagement, Shuffer's men recovered supplies, make the latter explanation more plausible. The reason why the 272nd was there mattered little to the American infantrymen, who found themselves under increasingly heavy fire. Shuffer tried to outflank the defenders early on with A Company, but his attempt to hook around the enemy left (on the western end of the line) was rebuffed by the defenders. The 272nd in turn tried to outflank Shuffer on his own left. In reply, Shuffer moved his own command group to the

Troops of 2-28th Infantry watch airstrikes being called in close proximity of the battalion's perimeter to break up the PLAF attacks during the second battle of Bau Bang. (US Army)

Colonel Brodbeck from Lai Khe inserted 1-16th Infantry by air assault in the hope of cutting off the troops attacking 2-28th. The assault did not cut off the whole enemy force, but forced the 272nd Regiment to withdraw while inflicting more losses on the PLAF unit. Troops from the 1-16th reported the enemy they encountered wore PAVN uniforms. At this stage of the war PLAF and PAVN units were more and more similar. (US Army)

On 8 June 1966 A Troop, 1-4th Cavalry moves through Lai Khe en route to An Loc. Just north of Chon Tanh the lead vehicle hit a mine halting the column and starting the battle of Ap Tau O. (US Army)

A M48A3 Patton tank of the 1-4th Cavalry. Due to generals Johnson and Westmoreland's misgivings, the Pattons of the 1st Infantry Division had been kept out of action. The battle at Ap Tau O was their first 'official' engagement. (US Army)

Reinforcements from the rest of 1-4th reach the scene after the conclusion of the fight. (US Army)

north, extending B Company's line to prevent it being outflanked. Still, enemy pressure forced B Company back. Shuffer now tried to consolidate a defensive perimeter, with C Company being its face toward the enemy, on the south side, B company holding the east side, A Company the west side and the battalion's command group the northern face.

If the 272nd thought it had the 2-2nd surrounded and primed for destruction, it had counted on neither the stubbornness of the American troops on the ground nor 3rd Brigade's flexibility in coordinating external firepower. Building on previous experiences, the 1st Infantry Division was in the process of devising procedures to provide simultaneous all-arms support. Colonels Brodbeck and Shuffer divided support by area and type. Within a few minutes, one divisional battery and one corps artillery battalion started to lay down fire in front of A and C Companies. The corps artillery unit was using self-propelled 175mm howitzers. Close air support was meanwhile directed on the area in front of B Company, while gunships soon supported the northern face of Shuffer's perimeter. By using separate, but close, target areas, Shuffer and Brodbeck were deconflicting air, helicopter and artillery support while using them in a coordinated fashion. The 272nd tried to negate supporting fire by closing the distance, but Shuffer's men stopped the enemy cold with their own fire.

Furthermore, instead of just hunkering down, as the 272nd seemed to expect, Shuffer – once the immediate crisis in front of B Company was averted – attacked southward with A and C Companies. Shuffer's aggressive push into the 272nd main defensive area doomed the defenders. By 1430 hours, Shuffer's men were deeply ensconced in the 272nd base camp, reducing it bunker by bunker. The 272nd started to give way, but tactical withdrawal soon gave way to a rout. The 272nd simply collapsed. By evening, Shuffer's men were the owners of the battlefield and of the 272nd's base camp. Not only bodies were recovered, but weapons, munitions and supplies. Shuffer's men counted 300 Viet Cong bodies in exchange for 39 of their own either killed or wounded. Far from having 'wiped out' an American battalion, the 272nd was forced to disappear for four months to rest and refit. Consequently, 1965 closed with a beaten and emaciated 9th PLAF Division leaving the field to Seaman's troops.

The new year brought the 25th Infantry Division to Chu Chi. The Big Red One spent January 1966 clearing and securing that location for the establishment of the 25th Division's base there. While large base camps, bunker systems and fortified positions were discovered in the area, no large-scale action resulted. Cam's PLAF division was still recovering from its November and December 'triumphs'. January also saw Operation CRIMP, a joint effort between the 1st Infantry Division and the 173rd Airborne. The enemy largely refused to fight, and no large units were engaged, with the majority of US losses being caused by mines. The 173rd Airborne (and its attached 1st Battalion, Royal Australian Regiment) engaged in several firefights, but not against large formations. Nevertheless, CRIMP uncovered and destroyed large base camps and supply areas. It also yielded important enemy documents that would immensely help MACV intelligence efforts. The amount of materiel captured or destroyed points toward hurried evacuations and the inability of the 9th PLAF Division to contest the operation.

Bau Bang again …

CRIMP was followed by MASTIFF, a two-brigade spoiling attack designed to thwart a possible attack by the 9th PLAF Division against ARVN positions. The operation did not produce any significant engagements. Colonel Brodbeck concluded that the 9th PLAF Division was shying away from major encounters, so he needed to entice the enemy with smaller targets. For Operation BOSTON/COCOA BEACH, he proposed to deploy single battalions rather than whole brigades in each sector. His target was the 272nd Regiment, reported by intelligence as resting in the general area of Bau Bang. In BOSTON/COCOA's framework, the 2-28th Infantry was engaged in a battalion sweep near Bau Bang on 3 March. The battalion has moved on foot from Lai Khe and established a defensive position just west of Bau Bang. They sent out several patrols from their battalion patrol base. The patrols discovered a kilometre-long trench, recently vacated. Lieutenant Colonel Kyle W. Bowie, the 2-28th's commander, took it as a sign the enemy was preparing something. He increased his patrols, and in the waning darkness of the early morning of 5 March, B Company, occupying the northern side of the battalion perimeter, heard noises from the north of their positions. A patrol led by 2nd Lieutenant Robert J. Hibbs went out and, thanks to starlight scope night vision, discovered an enemy supply column moving toward the perimeter. The column comprised armed soldiers, women and children. The women were carrying weapon bundles, while the children bore ammunition. The column stopped, allowing several women and children to leave, then continued toward the 2-28th perimeter. After the column passed Hibbs's position, he detonated two Claymore mines and the US troops lobbed grenades before scurrying back toward the battalion perimeter. They met another enemy force, possibly the one waiting resupply, and charged it. Hibbs was mortally wounded while charging two machine gun positions that barred the retreat of his patrol. He was later recommended for a Medal of Honor.

Hibbs's action spoiled the 272nd Regiment's attack timetable. Although his pursuers attacked first, they were repelled by concentrated small arms fire. The main assault started at approximately 0645 hours, with the first of a series of overlapping attacks from different directions. The attacks seemed to have been echeloned to force the Americans to move troops from one side of the perimeter to another, creating a weakness to be exploited later. Yet Bowie's men held firm, aided by the batteries at Lai Khe. In addition, USAF F-100s were soon on the scene, making several passes with 500lb bombs targeting enemy concentrations. Other Super Sabres dropped cluster bombs on the long trench discovered before the attack. While outnumbered, the 2-28th held firm. By mid-morning, the 272nd had had enough and withdrew.

At the same time, Colonel Brodbeck in Lai Khe inserted his second battalion, the 1-16th, by helicopter north-west of the 2-28th. With Bowie reporting a concentration of enemy attacks from that direction, Brodbeck hoped to put the withdrawing 272nd between his two battalions. The reinforcements encountered and brushed off a small force dressed in regular PAVN uniforms and reached Bowie at 1430 hours. Two hours before, a patrol from the 2-28th perimeter had spotted a company-sized enemy force deployed on the road from Lai Khe in an ambush position, as the 272nd expected American relief forces to come on foot. The enemy company was promptly subjected to an artillery barrage. The following day, Colonel Shuffer and his battalion also arrived on the scene, but no significant engagements occurred. However, plenty of bodies, weapons and equipment were collected. The first action of the 272nd after its enforced rest and refit had been another disaster. According to MACV, 199 enemy troops were killed against 15 Americans, six of whom were victims of a helicopter crash.

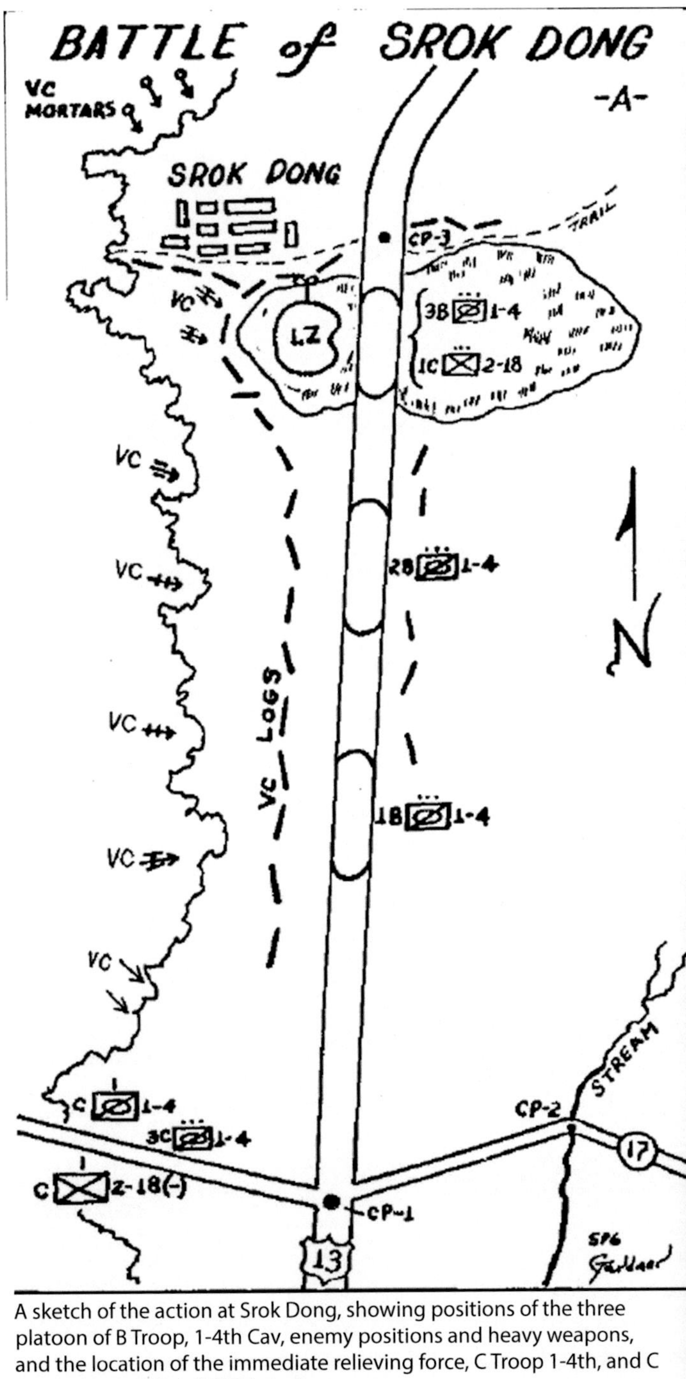

A sketch of the action at Srok Dong, showing positions of the three platoon of B Troop, 1-4th Cav, enemy positions and heavy weapons, and the location of the immediate relieving force, C Troop 1-4th, and C Company, 2-18th Inf. (US Army)

Ap Tau O, Pattons in the fight

On 8 June, General Johnson's concerns about the suitability of M48 Pattons for Vietnam were proven unfounded. That day, Colonel Brodbeck had ordered A Troop from the 1-4th Cavalry to An Loc. General DePuy at 1st Division HQ had received intelligence that the 9th PLAF Division was again on the offensive, intending to hit several towns along Highway 13: Loc Ninh, An Loc and Chon Thanh. Brodbeck's 3rd Brigade was already operating in the general area. The colonel was ordered to reinforce ARVN positions in these locales. Brodbeck's forces were reinforced too, and the colonel controlled a total of six infantry battalions.[13]

That morning, A Troop moved toward An Loc with nine M48 Pattons and 32 other vehicles, including two M132 flamethrowers.[14] ARVN troops were attached to the formation. During the afternoon, the column passed the hamlet of Ap Tau O. The leading M48 was hit by a RCL round or hit a mine on the road, immobilising the whole 3km-long column. Two battalions from the 272nd Regiment were in position and attacked the immobilised column, but the VC attacks were uncoordinated and poorly executed. Enemy small arms, RCL rounds and mortar shells hit various points of the column. A Troop coiled in a defensive perimeter, bringing all its weapons to bear. At times small groups of enemy soldiers rushed toward single vehicles, trying to plant satchel charges, only to be mowed down by American fire.

In addition to 90mm guns, machine guns, flamethrowers, small arms and mortars, A Troop's commander, Captain Ralph M. Sturgis, quickly called in artillery from Loc Ninh and air strikes. The 272nd Regiment continued to attack for around four hours but was unable to dent the defensive perimeter. In the meantime, Colonel Brodbeck used helicopters to move the 2-18th Infantry a few kilometres north of the ambush location. Once on the ground, the infantry battalion quickly moved south to the sound of the guns. The ARVN commander also reacted, sending elements of the 5th Infantry Division to the scene. The ambushers thus became the ambushed. The 272nd broke contact at the time the infantry was linking up with A Troop, leaving weapons and bodies on the scene. Allied troops recovered 105 enemy dead and estimated another 150–200 casualties.[15] Approximately 1,200 PLAF soldiers had attacked just 135 US and ARVN troopers, and were bloodily repulsed. The tanks had also proved their worth.

LTC Leonard L. Lewane, the CO of 1-4th Cavalry after the battle. Lewane flew over the battle area in his command helicopter coordinating air and artillery strikes and managing the reinforcing units. (US Army)

The Minh Than Road

The defeat at Ap Tau O did not deter Colonel Cam. The 9th PLAF Division was still committed to its summer offensive. In response, General DePuy brought to An Loc his 1st Brigade, under Colonel Sidney Berry. He also deployed the division's forward command post. This was a pattern that would be repeated later, during ATTLEBORO. Once DePuy assumed he had engaged the main enemy force, he quickly concentrated his whole division against it. Colonels Berry and Brodbeck translated DePuy's intentions into action in Operation EL PASO II, using their infantry battalions to scour the area around An Loc and beyond to find and fix the enemy. American battalions usually operated on the basis of radio finding or intelligence reports. Results were mixed. On 11 June, A Company, 2-28th Infantry of Brodbeck's 3rd Brigade and a CIDG platoon encountered the 1st Battalion of the 273rd Regiment in the area of Loc Ninh, north of An Loc. The 273rd Regiment contested two hills – Hills 150 and 177 – for 10 hours, but in vain. Lieutenant Colonel Bowie, the battalion commander, fed more infantry and fire support to overwhelm the enemy. At other times, American and South Vietnamese troops found only arms caches. By the end of the month, DePuy withdrew Colonel Berry's 1st Brigade, leaving Brodbeck's men scouring the area.

The troopers and vehicles of 1-4th Cavalry were again involved in a heavy fight on 30 June. This time losses were heavier, but the cavalry again prevailed. One of the key elements was the tempestive intervention of air strikes. O-1 observation planes were on the scene five minutes after the start of the battle allowing USAF Forward Air Controller to spot enemy support weapons and bring to bear air strikes. (US Army)

With Troop B pinned down by enemy fire, air strikes were instrumental. Eighty-eight close air support sorties were flown in support of the Troop. Here an F-100D from the 308TFS/31TFW is firing rockets in support of Big Red One's troopers. (US Army)

On 30 June, beside airpower, artillery was also instrumental in beating the 271st Regiment. Here the 155mm big guns of the 8-6th Artillery are firing in support. The battalion employed both towed M114A1 howitzers and self-propelled M109s. (US Army)

On 30 June, B and C Troops, 1-4th Cavalry, together with C Company, 2-18th Infantry, were escorting engineers to repair a bridge at Cam Le, between An Loc and Loc Ninh. The 1-4th's commanding officer, Lieutenant Colonel Leonard L. Lewane, was in charge of the convoy. The 271st Regiment was waiting for them, having created an L-shaped ambush position approximately 2km in length around the intersection between the QL 13 and a secondary road, Route 17. The regiment had been initially ordered to attack Loc Ninh, but its mission changed on 27 June from attacking the town to ambushing convoys on the road.[16] Lewane's troops entered the ambush at around 0940 hours, close to the hamlet of Srok Dong, with B Troop in the van. The troopers were taken under a deluge of mortar, recoilless rifle, machine gun and small arms fire. B Troop returned fire and pulled back toward the intersection of the two roads but was forced back again. Within 30 minutes, all of its M48 tanks had been disabled.[17] Up in his command and control helicopter, Colonel Lewane diverted an F-100 airstrike to support B Troop and called for gunships. He also dispatched his second troop, C Troop, to support B Troop. C Troop's tanks and APCs charged the ambush, with more air strikes and artillery support raining down upon the 271st Regiment. C Troop relieved B Troop, then took the brunt of the fight while their comrades withdrew south, reorganised and moved to the west to flank the ambush position. Around noon, the enemy started to withdraw, having had enough of the cavalry and its supporting fire. Allied reinforcements were also reaching the area. A CIDG company was deployed north of Srok Dong to block the enemy retreat, while elements of the ARVN 5th Infantry Division took up positions east of B Troop on Route 17. Colonel Brodbeck also dispatched his infantry companies to cordon the area. Lieutenant Colonel Herbert J. McChrystal's 2-18th took over the pursuit from the exhausted cavalry troopers. By 1615 hours, the 271st was in full retreat.

DePuy redeployed his 1st Brigade to An Loc, ordering Colonel Berry to take over at Srok Dong and engage in a vigorous pursuit of

Preparing for the move. Lt. John T. Lyons, commander of 1st Platoon, C Troop, 1-4th Cav is working on a ledger while awaiting the order to move. Note the M60 machine gun on the side of his M113. (US Army)

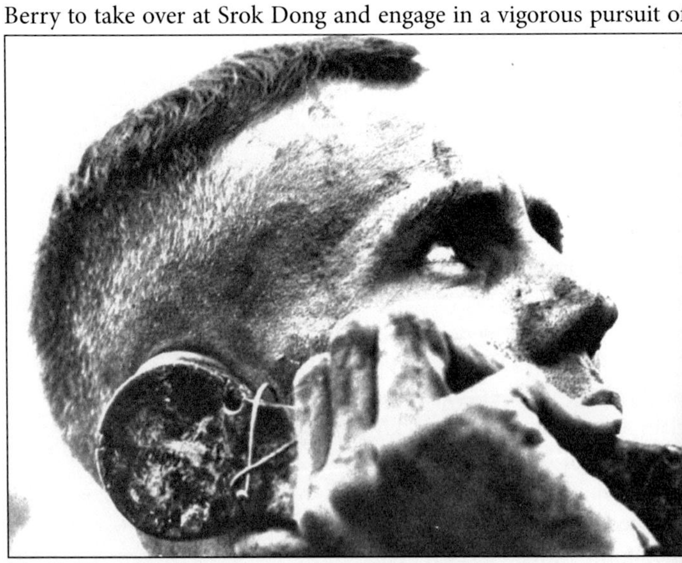

The link between fire support and the troops on the ground were the forward artillery observers and their USAF counterparts, the Forward Air Controllers. More than once survival of US troops depended on their competence, professionalism, and personal courage. (US Army)

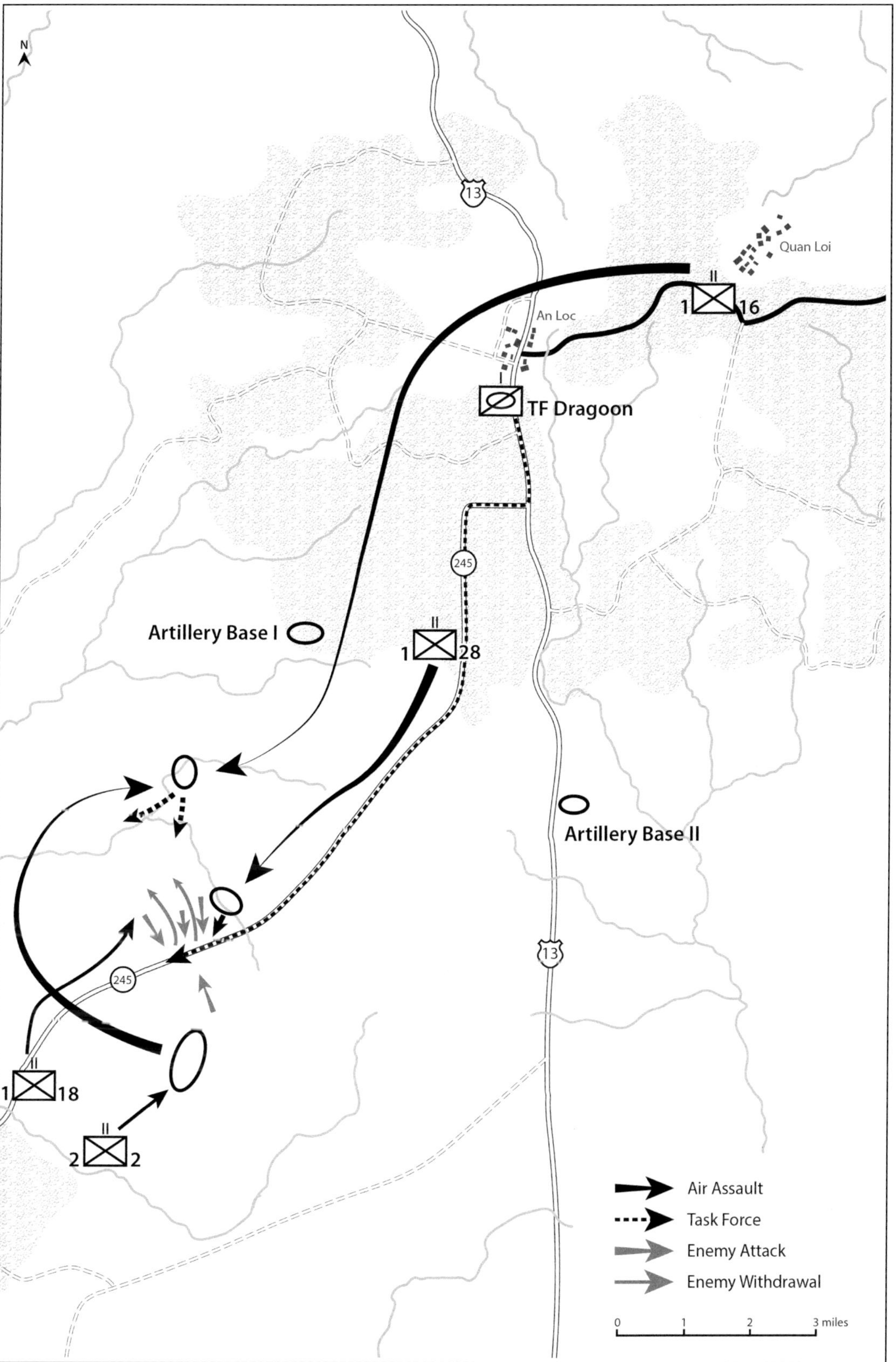

The concept of operations for what was called the battle of the Minh Thanh road. Task Force Dragoon simulated a convoy, while two artillery firebases had been created to provide continuous artillery support. Four infantry battalions were in position to be inserted in the battle to trap the wouldbe ambushers. (Map by George Anderson)

the 9th PLAF Division. Colonel Cam, on his part, threw the 273rd Regiment into the fray to cover the 271st. On 1 July, the 273rd attacked A Company, 2-18th Infantry near Ta Thiet. McChrystal responded by sending his reconnaissance platoon and C Company to support A Company in stopping the 273rd attack. After a lull in the night, the 273rd attacked the two companies at 0545 hours the following day. Initially, the US troops could not receive air support because of adverse weather, but as soon as this cleared, F-100s from Bien Hoa added their ordnance to the fire from the defenders. By 0900 hours, the PLAF regiment had had enough and pulled back. It had covered the retreat of its sister regiment, but at a considerable price.[18]

After Ta Thiet, the 9th PLAF Division largely avoided contact, prompting DePuy to devise a way to ambush the ambushers. He instructed Colonel Berry to create a fake convoy from An Loc to lure an enemy force into a prepared killing ground. Berry complied, using the 1-4th Cavalry as the bait. Task Force Dragon, comprising B and C Troop reinforced by B Company, 1-2nd Infantry, left An Loc on 9 July, escorting engineers to Minh Tanh to repair the airfield there. In a series of apparently unrelated moves, Berry deployed three artillery batteries with 105mm, 155mm and 8-in howitzers near the QL 13. Another 105mm battery deployed south of An Loc. The 2-2nd Infantry was deployed to Minh Than in small groups in the preceding days, reinforcing the 1-18th and an artillery battery there. In all, more than two infantry battalions, two cavalry troops and five artillery batteries were arrayed against a potential ambusher. Faithful to their playbook, the 272nd Regiment prepared a textbook L-shaped ambush along Route 245 between An Loc and Minh Thanh. They opened fire against C Troop at 1110 hours on 9 July.

American tanks and APCs quickly deployed in herringbone formation on both sides of the road and opened fire, while artillery rained steel on the ambushers. By 1230 hours, the 272nd realised that they had been ambushed by their opponents. While they were busy dealing with Task Force Dragon, Colonel Berry had deployed his infantry around the battle zone to trap the VC. Not only had the two battalions at Minh Thanh been used, but the 1-28th was also helicoptered from An Loc. A South Vietnamese cavalry troop also joined the battle. By the evening, the battle was over. While the 272nd was able to filter through the allied cordon, it paid a huge price. Berry's men recovered 238 enemies KIA,

Highway (Route Nationale/QL) 13 was nicknamed the Thunder Road because of the constant threat of ambushes. The 1st Infantry Division also used it to its own advantage as Task Force Dragoon did on 9 July. Here elements of the 1-4th Cavalry are preparing to move out. These are M113s with the Okinawa-manufactured shielded cupola for the commander's .50 machine gun, rather than the more usual ACAV rounded shields. (US Army)

The battle is joined. 1st Platoon, C Troop, 1-4th Cavalry comes under heavy fire and deploys. The fight raged at close quarters along the entire 1,200 metre length of the column. (US Army)

An infantryman from 1-18th Infantry moving toward the battalion's blocking position, finding the going difficult as the area along Route 245 was marshy. (US Army)

An M48 from 1-4th Cav at the start of the operation. The Cavalry is on the move. (US Army)

Forward Air Controllers were already over the column before the fight started. Captain John W. Harrison, flying in an O-1 was the first to spot the enemy. (Albert Grandolini)

Another element of support for the operation was a series of B-52 strikes launched the day before. Here a B-52F Hits a LZ near Sroc Con Trang, north of Artillery Base I. The strikes hit the 273rd Regiment hard. (USAF).

The bulk of air support on 9 July was provided by F-5Cs. They made passes firing their 20mm guns or dropping napalm. Napalm was considered the most effective weapons used by air in the engagement. Here three F-5Cs are in the arming area of Bien Hoa Air Base in 1966. The F-5s, under the 4503rd Tactical Fighter Squadron, were part of the F-100 equipped 3rd TFW. (USAF)

Beside jets, attack helicopters – in this case UH-1B gunships – also played an important part in mauling the 9th PLAF Division. Here three UH-1Bs armed with rockets are searching the jungle. (Albert Grandolini)

Three F5Cs from the 10th Tactical Fighter Squadron are taking turn to refuel from a KC-135. They carry Mk117 demolition bombs.

On the way! A 105mm howitzer from one of the two supporting firebases fires in support of Task Force Dragoon. Note the quantity of shells stacked close to the gun, and the empty cases already discarded. (US Army)

Colonel Sidney B. Berry the commander of 2nd Brigade, who planned and controlled Operation EL PASO II. (US Army)

and estimated another 300.[19] Prisoner interrogation later revealed that the 9th Division suffered heavily in the battles of June and July, claiming a reduction of 50 percent in the division's effectiveness.[20] The 9th Division admitted considerable losses for the 9 July action alone, with 128 killed and 167 wounded.[21] Yet losses were blamed on poor performance of regimental commanders, rather than US effectiveness.[22] After the battle, DePuy continued to keep the pressure on the 9th Division, but encounters with it became less and less frequent. Even the aggressive DePuy characterised his operations in August, September and October as of only limited success. On several occasions, his brigade and battalion commanders thought they had pinned large enemy units, but their hopes were dashed: the 9th PLAF Division did not offer battle.

According to the 9th PLAF, all encounters with the Americans, while costly, had produced significant successes. Cam's account of the 5 March engagement of the division's 272nd Regiment against the American 2-28th Infantry defensive position at Bau Bang reported a significant success that neutralised an entire enemy battalion.[23] Yet the reality was somewhat different, the 272nd being repulsed and inflicting very few casualties on Colonel Bowie's battalion. The action at Bau Bang was just one in a long string of encounters when Cam's assessment of his regiments' successes did not match the situation on the ground.

By all accounts, the 9th Division had been severely beaten in every single encounter with the 1st Infantry Division or other American formations in the area. The 9th Division was now nowhere to be found because it has been shredded to pieces. Yet its commander, at least in his reports, appeared confident that he was winning the 'big unit war' his superiors at COSVN had launched. The pressing question is how much of this confidence was just posturing and how much was the product of a reporting system that was, to put it mildly, abused by local commanders who fabricated incredible battlefield successes to justify the staggering losses they were suffering and, possibly, hide their own incompetence. US Army historian John Carland suggests that for all his bluster, Cam indeed realised his division was getting mauled. In the aftermath of the battles on the Minh Than road, Carland commented that the 9th Division was breaking contact with the 1st Infantry Division and directing its attention to a new target, the 196th Infantry Brigade, freshly arrived at Tay Ninh. Carland's comments suggest that Cam had come to the realisation that he was just playing into DePuy's hands and guns.[24] A similar reasoning could be seen, as will be discussed shortly, in Cam's own orders. Was the 9th Division losing its war against the Americans and DePuy?

5
ATTLEBORO

As has been discussed, in the face of what was, for all practical purposes, a strategic stalemate, both sides attempted to wrestle the initiative through an ambitious concept of offensive operations. By all accounts, by 1966, MACV had demonstrated it had a distinct firepower advantage over the communist forces. Despite the disingenuous claims in NLF and PAVN sources, American artillery, tanks and close air support were critical factors on the battlefield. More than that, they were something that neither NLF nor PAVN units were able to cope with. In addition, Westmoreland was introducing new allied combat units at an increased pace in preparation for his own offensive, which was designed to start in the III CTZ.

The 9th Division's autumn offensive: Target Tay Ninh?

Nevertheless, COSVN had not yet given up its focus on big unit battles and its strategy of attrition focused on the ARVN and other elements of Saigon's government. But COSVN started to recognise that to hit the ARVN, Americans had to be engaged first. More importantly, COSVN was ready to strike first. Continuing their policy to strike at the heart of South Vietnam's government, the ARVN, the communists decided to launch another ambitious scheme in the III CTZ. COSVN ordered Senior Colonel Hoang Cam and his 9th PLAF Division to launch a winter–spring offensive to:

> destroy a vital element of the enemy, support the local movement, oppose enemy pacification and expansion effort, break the oppressive government control, widen friendly liberated areas, and provide security and protection for storage facilities and base areas of Dung Minh Chau.[1]

This was a tall order for a unit that had suffered severe losses during the previous months.

Notwithstanding the condition of the 9th Division, offensive action was essential to kept pressure on allied forces in the III CTZ while they were massing in preparation for their own offensive operations. The alternative was either a risky offensive or just waiting for an even heavier American blow. The steady arrival of new American battalions had not escaped COSVN's notice. MACV's build-up was painfully evident to all. In less than a year, the area around Saigon had seen the arrival of two full infantry divisions, part of another and several independent units. If MACV was to strike, the III CTZ seemed the logical point. It was not just a result of force concentration; the area was indeed critical. Despite Saigon not being technically part of the III CTZ, it sat right in the middle of it. Securing the area around the capital was paramount, as, from the COSVN perspective, it was paramount to be able to continue to threaten it. The focus on this area had been clear from 1964. The HOP TAC plan, even if not successful, had focused on that specific area. In September 1966, it was clear to friend and foe that MACV would have made another effort there, this time using its newly assembled American forces. General Tanh was simply going to pre-empt that strike: Cam's battered division had to suffice.

Obviously, COSVN calculations were based on what they perceived as a successful campaign against US forces in the region. Colonel Cam had reported that his division's losses had been sustained in exchange for greater successes in weakening the enemy. His reports to COSVN and General Tanh had painted the clashes of the summer in a positive light. Yet, the continuous battles had only highlighted Tanh's preoccupation with the area. Even if 'thwarted', the Americans were exerting a constantly increasing pressure in the area, so an offensive was a logical response. Based on the previous reports, Tanh was expecting his forces to deliver another significant blow, hopefully a critical one. The 9th Division's autumn offensive was indeed an ambitious one. The overarching target was Tay Ninh city, the provincial capital. Successfully taking a district or, as in this case, a provincial, capital had always attracted both PLAF and

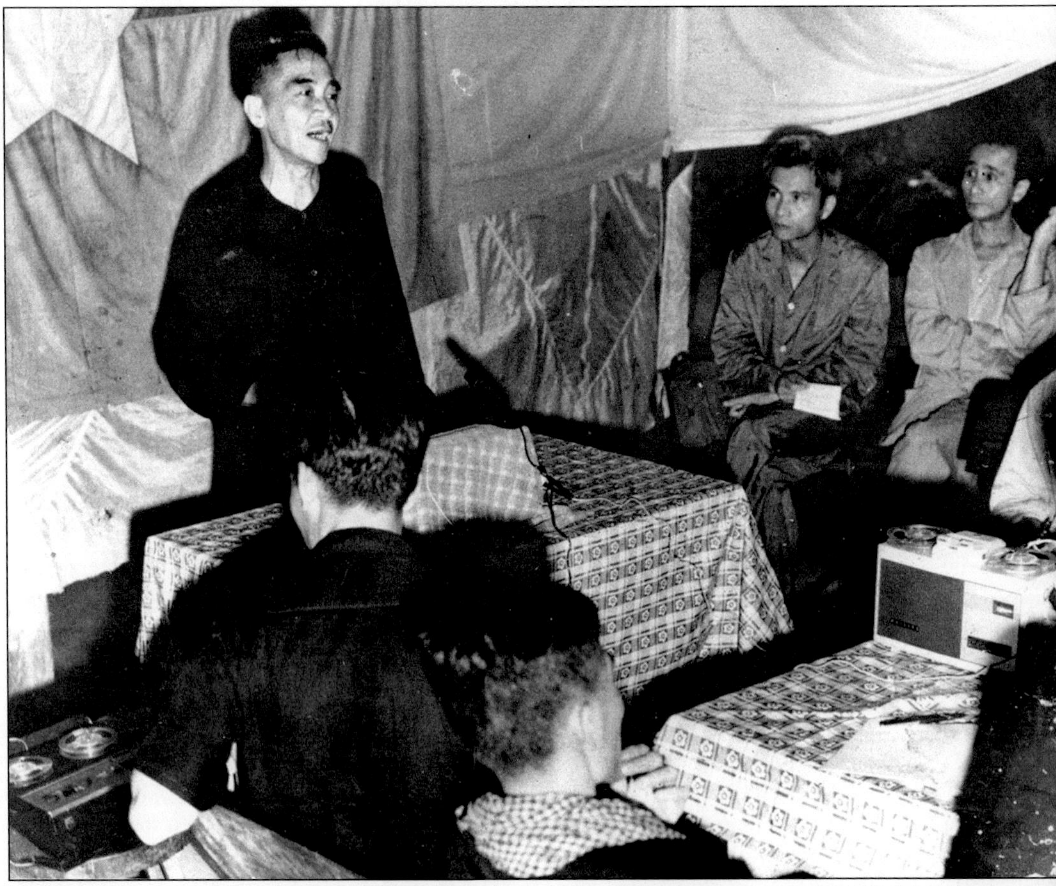

A meeting at the COSVN Headquarters in 1966. The officers in the picture have not been identified, but the presence of the recorder suggest the speaker is a senior political cadre or a political commissar. (Albert Grandolini)

To launch its offensive, the 9th PLAF Division needed supplies. Supplies were usually moved by truck in Cambodia and by porter either on foot or on bicycles as here in South Vietnam. These supplies were then placed in camouflaged supply caches to be distributed to combat units. The discovery of large supply caches started Operation ATTLEBORO. (Albert Grandolini)

PAVN forces. Tay Ninh was protected by ARVN troops and the newly arrived US 196th Light Infantry Brigade. If he wanted to strike the ARVN garrison and take the city, he had to deal with the Americans first. Even if the 9th Division could not take the city itself, causing significant losses to the enemy would have set their operations back. The 196th also appeared a more manageable opponent than DePuy's battle hardened Big Red One. The brigade had only just arrived in the region and lacked the lavish support of the 1st Infantry Division.

To fulfil his mission, Cam asked for and obtained additional resources from COSVN, which directed the neighbouring 7th PAVN Division to detach the 101st Regiment to reinforce the 9th Division. Why a division that was supposedly routinely defeating the American invaders needed a full infantry regiment as reinforcement is never explained in COSVN documents. Cam also complained that the 101st was a green unit and needed more training and his own close supervision.[2] For that reason, Cam attached himself to the regiment. Criticism of the 101st, warranted or not, was a common thread of Cam's account of the whole subsequent battle. Cam's misgiving about the reinforcements aside, the 9th Division appeared reasonably ready for the upcoming battle, so long as it was fought on Cam's terms and within his force estimates.

Cam's concept of operations was based on three separate regiment-size attacks. The first one was to fall on Tay Ninh and the 196th Infantry Brigade on 3 November, a task assigned to the 271st Regiment. After the main attack, the regiment was expected to lure out and destroy American reaction forces. Two battalions of the battered 272nd Regiment, supported by the 14th Local Force Battalion, were also to attack government outposts at Suoi Cao, 30km south of Tay Ninh. Finally, the last battalion of the 272nd and the whole 101st PAVN Regiment, from the 7th Division, were to deliver the centrepiece of the plan, an attack against the CIDG camp at Suoi Da, 15km north-east of Tay Ninh. The attack force was supported by anti-aircraft units and a mortar company from Cam's division. One fixture of communist planning in the early phase of the American intervention in Vietnam was the use of Special Forces camps as bait to lure out relief forces and then ambush and destroy them. If everything had followed the script, ARVN and US forces in the province would have been severely weakened and Tay Ninh would have been left vulnerable. This would have prevented further offensives and accomplished the goal of protecting local supply and storage areas.

Decades on from the battles, it is difficult to ascertain just how much Cam believed in his own successes and how much his reports had been written only to please his superiors, but later references to unrealistic reporting is telling. On the other hand, there are no indications that he expected significant interference from the 1st Infantry Division in the upcoming offensive and he discounted enemy reinforcements from nearby provinces. Overall, his concept of operations for the upcoming offensive betrayed a reluctance to engage the Big Red One again. The main target for his November offensive was the 196th Light Infantry Brigade, just settling into its new base at Tay Ninh. Cam claimed the American unit was inexperienced and not yet ready to fight.[3] He clearly wanted an easy target. The other geographical targets were several CIDG camps. These camps had always been a favourite target of PLAF and PAVN attacks. Not only were the camps themselves not designed to repel large-scale conventional assaults, but their own vulnerability to such attacks had often prompted commanders in Saigon – be they American or South Vietnamese – to dispatch relief forces, often from the elite Airborne or Marine divisions, the only general reserve available to the South Vietnamese government. In turn, these relief expeditions had provided the communists with the chance to ambush and maul these units.

A typical case was the December 1964 engagement at Binh Gia, where an attack on a village held by Catholic militias had sparked a prolonged, division-size battle that had mauled several elite ARVN battalions.[4] Binh Gia had not been an isolated case. However, these tactics could backfire spectacularly. The November 1965 attacks at Plei Me and Duc Co had proven that ARVN relief columns were not the easy targets that COSVN assumed. Once engaged, the ambushing forces were fixed in place. In the Pleiku area this precipitated a series of engagements with the 1st Cavalry Division that effectively crippled the PAVN 325C Division. In the III CTZ, Cam's own ambushes had resulted in the Big Red One mauling the 9th Division. Yet Cam had not been a witness to the Ia Drang battles, and his reports of the spring and summer battles painted a picture of destroyed US battalions and PLAF triumphs.

There is another element in the 9th Division plan that needs to be addressed. For all his bluster about defeating American forces in the summer, Cam's plan indeed reflected the traditional priorities of COSVN, targeting RVN forces being the primary objective. The 196th Infantry Brigade was just an inconvenience to be dealt with to damage the South Vietnamese Army and Saigon's government. The Americans had to be engaged to prevent their interference further down the plan. The distribution of the forces involved is revealing.

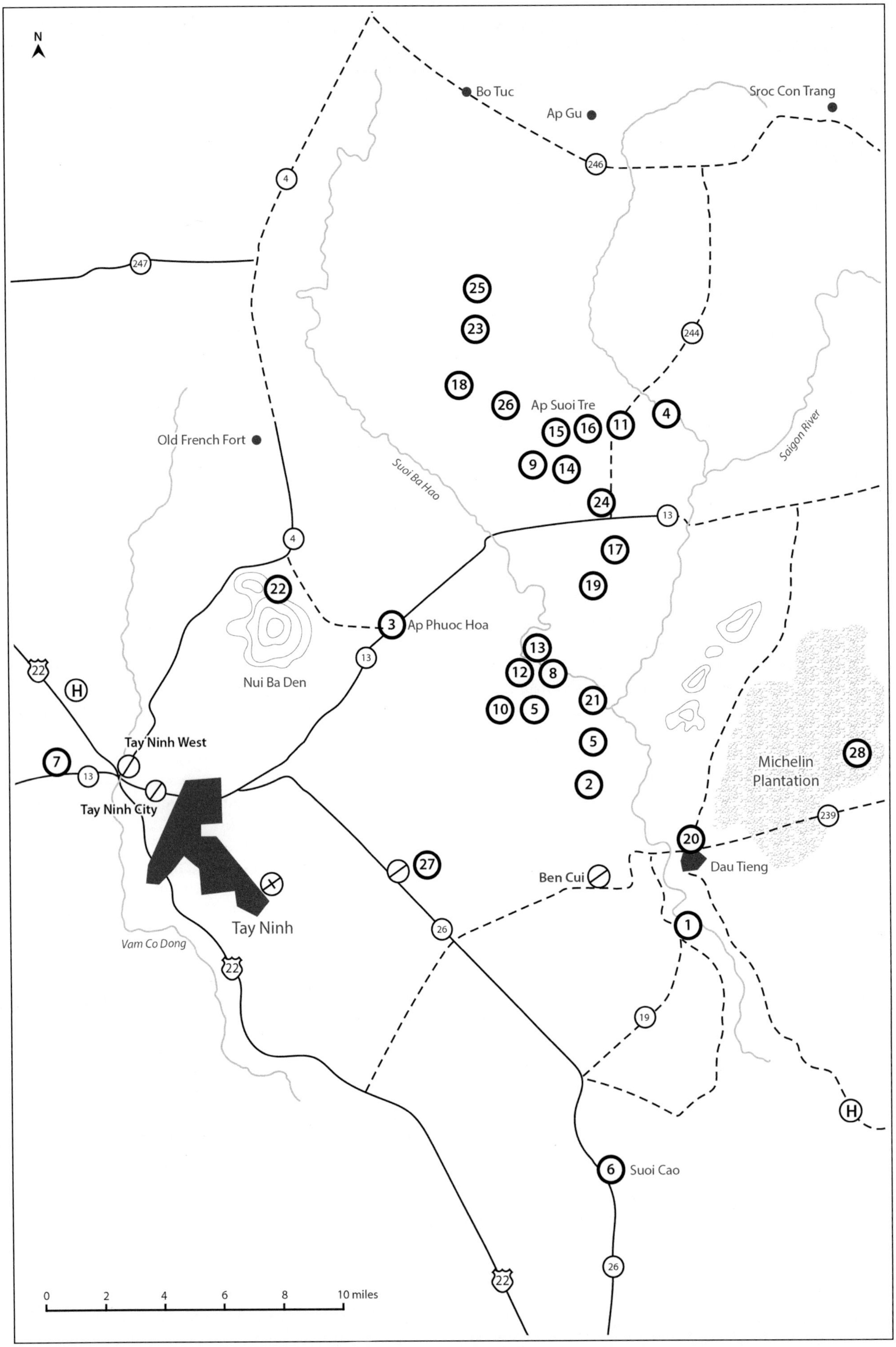

An overview of Operation ATTLEBORO with key events. (Map by George Anderson)

Operation ATTLEBORO: Key Events

1. 26 September: large rice store captured (279 tons).
2. 31 October: large rice store captured (843 tons).
3. 4 November: Suoi Da Special Forces Camp reinforced by Mike Forces.
4. 3 November: Mike Forces contact with the enemy.
5. 3 November: 196th LIB Landing Zones.
6. 4 November: attack on Suoi Cao.
7. 4 November: Tay Ninh attacked by mortar fire.
8. 4 November: 1-27th Engages the PAVN 101st Regiment.
9. 4 November: Mike Forces discover enemy base camp and are heavily engaged. They will be overrun the following day.
10. 5 November: Task Force 1-27th under attack for the whole day.
11. 6 November: Mike Force contact with a VC platoon.
12. 6 November: 2-28th lands in support of Task Force 1-27th under heavy covering air strikes. Two large enemy base camps are captured.
13. 7 November: more enemy base camps are captured and 70 enemy bodies are recovered, probably killed by air and artillery strikes.
14. 8 November: 1-28th attacked.
15. 8 November: 2-16th and 2-28th captures a large enemy base camp and find enemy bodies in a fresh grave.
16. 9 November 2-28th find 85 bodies in a tunnel and another 10 in the open.
17. 10 November: 2-16th finds another large base camp this one held by the PAVN 101st Regiment's camp captured.
18. 11 November: 1-18th finds and destroy another base camp.
19. 11 November: 2-16th finds a base camp, the camp is destroyed by airstrikes.
20. 12 November: Dau Tieng hit by mortar rounds.
21. 13 November: 1-26th Captures 358 tons of rice.
22. 14 November: 4-31st find enemy in caves at Nui Ba Den, airstrikes called.
23. 15 November: 2-18th lands under fire, air and helicopter strikes are called in. Three helicopters are shot down.
24. 16 November: 1-26th captures 620 tons of rice and 17 tons of salt.
25. 16 November: 2-18th in contact with an enemy platoon.
26. 17 November: 2-28th discovers major enemy base camp.
27. 18 November: 2-1st engages 20 enemy.
28. 18 November: 1-503rd engages an enemy platoon.

The 271st and 272nd Regiments deployed around 1,500 men in each of their attacks, while the 101st PAVN Regiment could count on more than 3,000 men. At this stage of the war, the Americans did not figure prominently in COSVN strategy, contradicting some claims that the communists had already divined the supposed American intolerance of casualties.[5] The plan also shows the typical weakness of PAVN and PLAF operations, namely the inability to cope with the capacity of US forces to quickly intervene on the battlefield and reinforce threatened positions. Neither Cam nor his superiors seemed to have planned for any US reaction except for walking into planned ambushes.

ATTLEBORO starts

Cam's plans unravelled quite quickly. Notwithstanding all the planning made both at COSVN and MACV, the Americans ended up striking first by mere chance. Contrary to Cam's expectations, the 196th Brigade did not lock itself in Tay Ninh. While settling his troops in Tay Ninh city, General De Saussure wanted to give his forces some actual combat and patrol experience, and not just use them in base-building tasks. To give the brigade some 'action', De Saussure launched Operation ATTLEBORO on 14 September, which initially consisted of battalion-sized probes around Tay Ninh itself. His approach was to use one battalion in the field while two worked at the base and rotate them to slowly introduce them to operational conditions. It appeared a reasonable course of action and was not expected to bring about any general engagement. Nothing in MACV, II Field Force or 196th Brigade documents and reports indicate any advance warning of the impending enemy offensive. At the start, ATTLEBORO was a purely routine operation.

Routine or not, ATTLEBORO yielded early results. During a completely unrelated operation, troops from the 25th Infantry Division had discovered a large rice cache toward the end of September, approximately 30km south-east of Tay Ninh. The 25th Infantry Division commander, General Weyand, asked De Saussure to extend his own operation farther east, hoping to capitalise on this initial discovery. The 196th Brigade commander promptly complied and, by mid-October, De Saussure's battalions were expanding the area of their operations. On 19 October, one of the brigade's battalions, 2-1st Infantry, moved into Dau Tieng and started to reconnoitre the area. On 23 October, the unit found a large rice cache north of the small town in several sheds. In the following days, similar finds were made. The 196th had stumbled on something. De Saussure reacted quickly to the discoveries. He asked permission to move his command post to Dau Tieng and for authority to increase the scope of his operation. Weyand was not in Chu Chi, having temporarily replaced General Seaman at the helm of II FFV. His deputy, Brigadier General George C. O'Connor, agreed with De Saussure's request. Destroying enemy supply areas fully fitted in with the 25th Infantry Division's concept of pacification: depriving the enemy of prepositioned supplies would force his main force units to disperse or move out of the area, freeing more of the division's resource for traditional COIN missions. At Bien Hoa, II FFV HQ, Weyand readily agreed.

De Saussure upgraded ATTLEBORO to a brigade-size operation on 30 October, shifted the 4-31st Infantry from Tay Ninh to Dau

Elements of 1-27th Infantry are welcomed at Bien Hoa Air Base by General Seaman on their arrival from Hawaii in January. While the 25th Division was deploying it was put under control of Seaman's 1st Infantry Division. A few months later the same men would bear the brunt of the action at Dau Tieng. (US Army)

PAVN and PLAF attacks relied on meticulous advance planning. Here troops are studying a model of a triangular Special Forces camp like those at Suoi Da and Suoi Cao. This kind of advance planning was a necessity due to the lack of battlefield communications. The drawback was a complete lack of either flexibility or the ability to react to unexpected situations. (Albert Grandolini

September 1966, elements of B Company, 2-27th Infantry land from their UH-1Ds for a search and destroy operation west of Saigon. (US Army)

Even if the big helicopters would have been readily available, moving rice was not an easy task. Usually, rice was stored in underground pits and had to be bagged before transportation. In three days, only 120 tons of rice had been moved. At the same time, the patrolling battalions uncovered signs that the enemy was preparing something. Earlier in the operation, on 23 October, children at Dau Tieng had reported 1,000 Viet Cong in the area.[6] Enemy attacks, usually with mortars, increased in the following days. On 28 October, the 2-1st Infantry found field obstacles in a village inhabited only by women and children. The women claimed the VC had forced them to dig the obstacles. Then a patrol discovered a document belonging to the 82nd Rear Service Group, War Zone C's main supply unit. The document revealed the presence of additional supply bases, but also that enemy forces were preparing to defend the area.[7]

These events alarmed O'Connor in Chu Chi. On 1 November, he ordered De Saussure to speed up operations and destroy rice caches in place rather than evacuating them. The 25th Division wanted to disrupt the enemy's supply network before its forces ensconced themselves in the area, but was not eager for a general engagement. As a precautionary measure, O'Connor reinforced De Saussure with the 1-27th Infantry from the 25th Infantry Division's 2nd Brigade. The same day, the 2-1st sustained three KIA during a contact with enemy forces defending a supply cache. After an uneventful 2 November, De Saussure decided the following day to deploy two

Thien and moved his personal command post to Dau Tieng. With the brigade main base at Tay Ninh still incomplete, the general stayed at Dau Tieng by day and flew back to Tay Ninh at night to check the situation there. By then, the troops had uncovered 843 tons of rice, a significant haul. The quantity of rice discovered, and its location, posed problems. The area was far from the road network, and helicopters were the only way to move significant loads. Such quantities could be moved only by Chinook, and even the CH-47 required several flights. Furthermore, Chinooks were still in short supply in Vietnam.

of his battalions, the 2-1st and the 4-31st, in a complex manoeuvre, hoping to uncover more supply depots. Two companies, B and C of the 1-27th, were to act as blocking forces. The Wolfhounds, the 27th Regiment's nickname, were to be airlifted into two separate blocking positions north of the Ba Hao stream, one company per position. At the same time, the two other battalions moved on four separate axes toward the stop line created by the stream.[8] The three battalions were divided in six, not mutually supporting, scattered forces. Reserves would be provided by the remaining company of the 1-27th at Dau

September 1966, members of B Company, 2-27th Infantry participated in a search and destroy operation west of Saigon in cooperation with ARVN units. US soldiers wears helmet covers while ARVN troops do not. (US Army)

Tieng and the 3-21st Infantry at Tay Ninh. On paper, the plan was complex; in reality, it was nightmarish.

There were no link up provisions and the units had no time to scout the terrain.[9] Even worse, the two companies of the 1-27th were basically left alone and isolated. The plan quickly fell apart. Major Guy S. Meloy, the young commander of the 1-27th, protested with General de Saussure when briefed on the evening of 2 November. Meloy had already served six months in Vietnam as an advisor to the ARVN airborne brigade. Yet he was just a major on the promotion list to lieutenant colonel, and De Saussure was a general. The plan was, as Meloy would later describe, ludicrous. The two blocking companies were 10km apart, in a triple-canopy forest where 500 metres per hour represented a good speed. The two advancing battalions were supposed to move between the blocking positions.[10]

Meloy's ordeal, 3–5 November

On 3 November, De Saussure's complicated choreography began. The 1-27th was airlifted into the two blocking positions without enemy interference, but then everything started to fall apart. C Company, in the western blocking position, began to receive fire at 1040 hours. Enemy forces, reported to be an entrenched infantry platoon, were attacked at 1206 hours.[11] The VC would later be identified as the 9th PLAF Division reconnaissance company, moving to screen the deployment of the 101st PAVN Regiment.[12] The enemy withdrew, but kept C Company under constant fire. C Company lost six killed and 14 wounded. Among the wounded were Captain Henderson, C Company's CO, and his company sergeant. An attempt was made to evacuate casualties, but enemy fire drove off the MEDEVAC helicopters. B Company had in the meantime discovered a base camp at 1207 hours, reporting that it had housed at least two enemy companies. With his C Company under fire, Major Meloy – orbiting the area in his command and control Huey – made his 'Dumb decision No. 1'. He ordered the pilot to fly low and slow over the C Company perimeter so he and his command group could literally jump out. Once on the ground, Meloy realised both the company commander and his sergeant were mortally wounded, and, in what he called Dumb Decision No. 2', he asked for another MEDEVAC mission.[13] A Huey from the 116th Assault Aviation Company, with volunteer pilots, was shot down over the perimeter when it was coming in to land. Of the crew of four, one crew chief was killed and the other wounded, but the two pilots were uninjured. Captain Henderson and his sergeant died immediately after the Huey crashed. Once settled on the ground, Meloy realised the precarious position of C Company and immediately called for reinforcements. B Company was ordered to move overland from its blocking position, with A Company, in reserve at Dau Tieng, to be airlifted into the LZ.

Orbiting over the battlefield, De Saussure inserted himself into the fight and countermanded Meloy's order to B Company. He did not explain his decision to Meloy, but it probably had to do with the timing of such an overland manoeuvre. Instead, De Saussure ordered his brigade reserve, the 3-21st at Tay Ninh, to move its C Company by helicopter to reinforce the Wolfhounds. On top of that, but without informing Meloy, he directed helicopters to lift B and C companies from 2-1st to reinforce Meloy. While the move was sound, the omission of informing the senior officer on the ground, Meloy, was an error, and one that De Saussure would repeat several times.[14]

While Meloy had no inkling of the scale of the reinforcements until they showed up, he was quick to deploy them. The battered C Company, 1-27th, went into reserve, while A Company, 1-27th, and C Company, 3-21st, enveloped and captured the enemy base camp. The two companies from the 2-1st were used to extend the defensive perimeter. By nightfall, Meloy had consolidated his force in a solid perimeter. At the same time, De Saussure had grouped the remainder of his 'searching' forces under Colonel Hugh H. Lynch, CO of the 4-31st, in another night laager several kilometres to the east. The situation now appeared under control. De Saussure had orbited the battlefield for most of the day, playing an instrumental role in bringing resupply and coordinating fire support. He then left for the night to plan his actions for the next day. His priority appears to have been to unscramble his forces and resume his search operation.[15]

Meanwhile, Colonel Cam was also reassessing his position and plans. Once informed of the American incursion, he scaled down his planned attacks and focused his attention on Meloy's mixed force: he would now destroy the 196th Infantry Brigade near Dau Tieng rather than at Tay Ninh.[16] The attacks at Tay Ninh and Suoi Cao became mere diversions. The attack against Suoi Da Special Forces Camp was cancelled. The main effort was to be north-west of Dau Tieng, and forces were summoned and repositioned accordingly. The 101st PAVN Regiment was to carry the brunt of the attack.

The following day, 4 November, De Saussure resumed his operation. In the morning, Meloy recalled:

> [T]he assistant Brigade S3 appeared at my command post with a map. The 2-1st companies were supposed to move overland some three kilometres and resume their attack on the red axis. I was to attack northeast to an arbitrary location along Route 9, the so-called Ghost Trail, and link up with my B Company which would attack west from its present position.[17]

Major Meloy had the two companies from the 2-1st move out once the morning fog lifted and started his own advance two hours later. His companies soon ran into a line of enemy bunkers in a well-prepared position. Post-battle surveys found several concrete bunkers, while even log bunkers were well constructed and had ample overhead protection to reduce the impact of artillery rounds. The bunkers were connected with covered passages and underground tunnels. The line was also well manned. During the night, Colonel Cam had been able to rush the 2nd Battalion of the 101st PAVN Regiment into position. He had instructed his forces to hold fire until the US troops were inside the woods. Meloy's force had hit a solid defensive line. His first reaction was to outflank and envelop the enemy, but his attempts to push companies to his right and left failed. Both flanking companies

Preparing for a heliborne assault. Here troops from the 1st Infantry Division prepare to board their Huey before an air assault. The men of 1-27th would have done much the same before the battle of Dau Tieng. (US Army)

A Soviet-made DHSK heavy machine gun used in anti-aircraft role. The weapons made helicopter landing close to the 1-27th's position extremely dangerous and led to losses. Major Meloy was forced to cut another landing zone to allow safer landings. (Albert Grandolini)

were pinned by enemy fire. Calls for artillery support did not produce an appreciable slackening in the enemy volume of fire.[18] Not only had his force been stopped, but it was taking casualties. The three line companies were affected, along with Meloy's command group. Soon everyone in his command group but a single radio operator had been wounded.[19]

Compounding Meloy's woes, the terrain and vegetation blocked radio contact with Brigade HQ at Dau Tieng. The situation improved after the 1-27th's S3 officer commandeered a helicopter to act as radio relay, USAF FACs acted as an intermediate station and Meloy's operation sergeant braved enemy machine gun fire to raise an antenna over the tree canopy. Once communications were restored, Meloy had no option but to call for reinforcements. Despite artillery support, he was unable to advance, while enemy fire prevented him from retreating.

The first help came from the two 2-1st companies. They stopped their original advance when hearing gunfire less than a kilometre away and quickly marched to the sound of battle. A and B Company of the 2-1st took casualties but were able to link up with Meloy during the afternoon. Captain Garret's B Company, 1-27th, also advanced toward the firefight, having spent the night in Colonel Lynch's laager and set out in the morning to rejoin its battalion. It even ambushed a PAVN platoon that was moving toward Meloy's position, but then – again without warning Meloy or providing any explanation – De Saussure ordered Garrett to rejoin Colonel Lynch's force. In its place, De Saussure sent C Company, 2-27th, from Dau Tieng. A Company, 2-27th, had been deployed to Dau Tieng with the battalion command group during the night on orders of General O'Connor, to support and reinforce De Saussure after the initial contacts. O'Connor had also moved C Company, 2-27th, during the morning, and promised the third company to De Saussure in case the situation worsened. C Company landed at Dau Tieng at 1100 hours and was alerted for possible employment in support of the 1-27th, together with the battalion command group, at 1246 hours. Lieutenant Colonel William C. Barrott, the 2-27th's commander, was personally briefed by De Saussure at Dau Tieng at 1420 hours. De Saussure wanted C Company to reach the general area of the engagement by helicopter and quickly move to join Meloy's left flank. Colonel Barrott requested that his A Company, then securing a helicopter crash site, to also deploy, but De Saussure ruled out that option.[20]

Barrott, his command group and C Company boarded helicopters and left Dau Tieng at 1440 hours. At the same time, the 2-27th Battalion S3, after having returned A Company to Dau Tieng, took a Huey helicopter to provide a radio link over the battle area. He and Barrott argued that A Company should be committed to the battle at that time in support of C Company, but De Saussure denied the request. Ten minutes before reaching the intended LZ, Barrott contacted Meloy. It was the first inkling the latter had of the deployment of C Company of the 2-27th. According to the 2-27th, it was 1515 hours.[21] Meloy instructed Barrott to land at an LZ 2km west of his position, then advance due east until a clearing and turn north. The message was possibly misunderstood, because Barrott led C Company first north and then east.[22] While Barrott and his men were moving toward Meloy, De Saussure apparently changed his mind about A Company and ordered it to airlift in the proximity of the 1-27th.[23] Barrott had ruled out the possibility of linking his own two companies around 1600 hours. C Company was deep in the woods and a link up with the fresh company appeared remote. Earlier in the operation, Meloy had reckoned that at best an infantry company was able to move around 500 metres per hour in the dense woods.[24] It was better for A Company to link up directly with Meloy.

Then disaster struck. C Company, 2-27th, had been under fire from its landing onward. While trying to reach the 1-27th's perimeter, Barrott and his men found themselves directly opposite to the bulk of the 101st PAVN Regiment. At 1715 hours, Captain Currer, C Company's CO, was killed while leading an assault on a machine gun bunker. Shortly afterward, Colonel Barrott threw a smoke grenade toward the 1-27th's lines. He and his force were not where Meloy supposed them to be, but very close to the perimeter, around 100 metres away. They were actually so close that artillery fire was hampered, and even firing in their general direction could be dangerous.[25] Colonel Barrott was killed around 1800 hours leading a charge against another machine

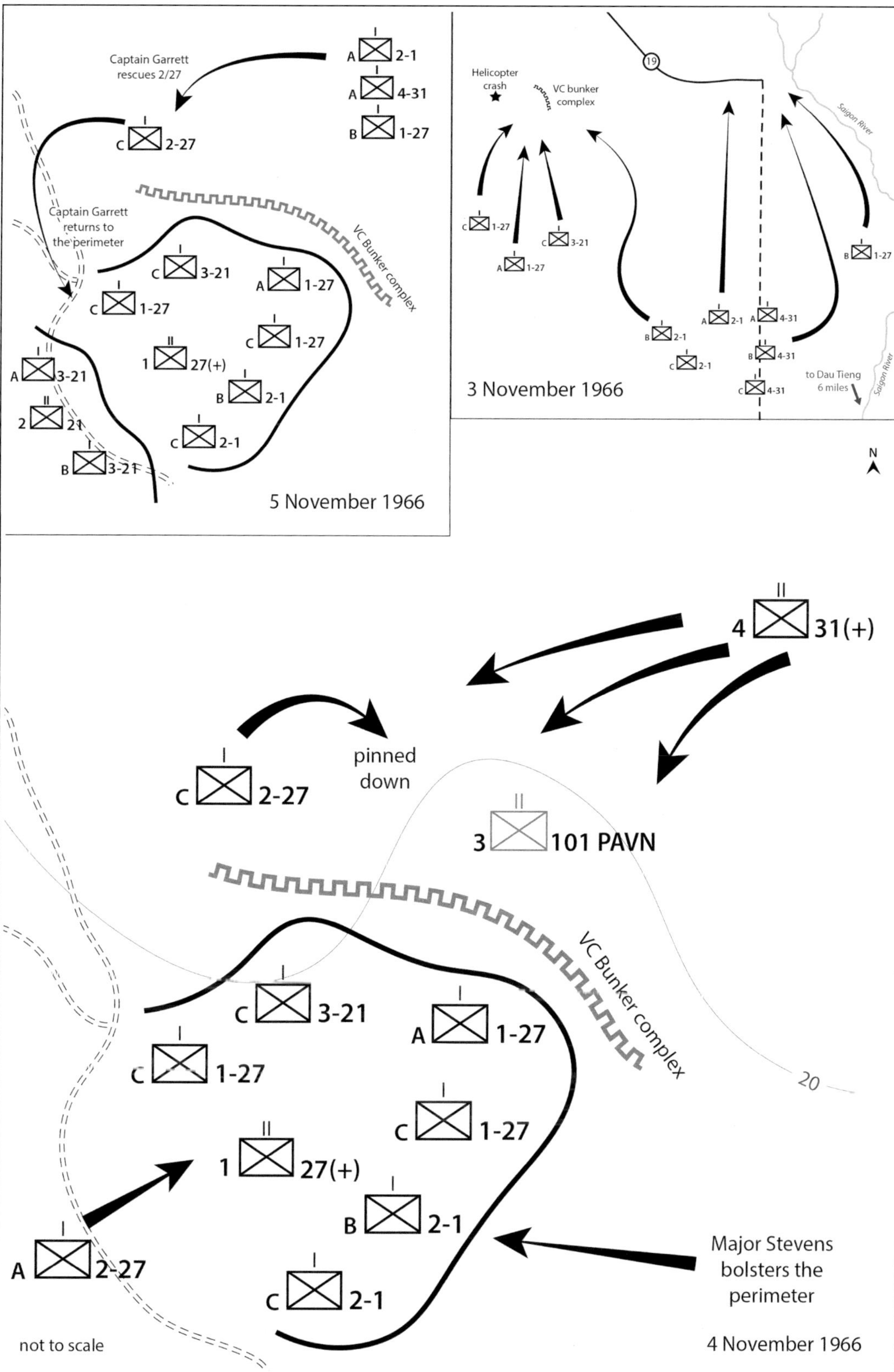

A map of the battle of Dau Tieng, based on an article written by then Major General Meloy. The map shows the movement in search of the enemy on the day before the action, and the two days of battles. (Map by George Anderson)

gun bunker while trying to reach Meloy's lines. Men from C Company twice tried to recover his body but failed.[26] At this time, Meloy was contacted by PFC Wallce, a radio operator in C Company, 2-27th, who apprised him of the dire situation. Not only had their attempt to break in failed, but they were unable to withdraw due to excessive casualties and lack of men to move them.[27]

Several hours after the start of the action, the American situation appeared on the verge of collapse. Meloy's task force was pinned in front of the enemy trenches and bunker, and unable to support C Company, 2-27th, which was now isolated behind them. Artillery and air support had failed to break the enemy, which at this point consisted of the bulk of the 101st Regiment. The only bright spot was the arrival of A Company, 2-27th. They entered the perimeter unopposed from the west and were able to clear a landing zone. Meloy could now evacuate his wounded, who had piled up during the day, and bring in resupply, mainly water, ammunition and medical supplies. That allowed him not only to hold during the night, but to attempt two attacks to relieve C Company. The men of the 1-27th, 2-1st and 3-21st still had plenty of fight in them. C Company of the 2-1st attacked first during the night, aiming at what was assumed to be a gap in the enemy lines, but the assault failed with five KIA and eight wounded.[28] At first light it was the turn of Captain Robert Foley's A Company, 2-27th. Foley and his men moved forward to rescue their comrades:

> Moving through the dense jungle to aid the besieged unit, Company A encountered a strong enemy force occupying well concealed, defensive positions, and the company's leading element quickly sustained several casualties. Capt. Foley immediately ran forward to the scene of the most intense action to direct the company's efforts. Deploying 1 platoon on the flank, he led the other 2 platoons in an attack on the enemy in the face of intense fire. During this action both radio operators accompanying him were wounded. At grave risk to himself he defied the enemy's murderous fire, and helped the wounded operators to a position where they could receive medical care. As he moved forward again one of his machine gun crews was wounded. Seizing the weapon, he charged forward firing the machine gun, shouting orders and rallying his men, thus maintaining the momentum of the attack. Under increasingly heavy enemy fire he ordered his assistant to take cover and, alone,

Capt. Foley continued to advance firing the machine gun until the wounded had been evacuated and the attack in this area could be resumed. When movement on the other flank was halted by the enemy's fanatical defense, Capt. Foley moved to personally direct this critical phase of the battle. Leading the renewed effort he was blown off his feet and wounded by an enemy grenade. Despite his painful wounds he refused medical aid and persevered in the forefront of the attack on the enemy redoubt. He led the assault on several enemy gun emplacements and, single-handedly, destroyed three such positions.[29]

On the night of 4 November, with the outcome of the battle of Dau Tieng still in doubt, elements of the 1st Infantry Division started to deploy. Here element of the division's 3rd Brigade are being airlifted at the Suoi Da Special Forces Camp. (US Army)

Captain Foley, rewarded with a Congressional Medal of Honor for his actions, was not alone in displaying personal bravery above and beyond the call of duty. Private John F. Baker (later promoted to sergeant) also received a Medal of Honor:

> For conspicuous gallantry and intrepidity in action at the risk of his life above and beyond the call of duty. En route to assist another unit that was engaged with the enemy, Company A came under intense enemy fire and the lead man was killed instantly. Sgt. Baker immediately moved to the head of the column and together with another soldier knocked out two enemy bunkers. When his comrade was mortally wounded, Sgt. Baker, spotting four Viet Cong snipers, killed all of them, evacuated the fallen soldier and returned to lead repeated assaults against the enemy positions, killing several more Viet Cong. Moving to attack two additional enemy bunkers, he and another soldier drew intense enemy fire and Sgt. Baker was blown from his feet by an enemy grenade. He quickly recovered and single-handedly destroyed one bunker before the other soldier was wounded. Seizing his fallen comrade's machine gun, Sgt. Baker charged through the deadly fusillade to silence the other bunker. He evacuated his comrade, replenished his ammunition and returned to the forefront to brave the enemy fire and continue the fight. When the forward element was ordered to withdraw, he carried one wounded man to the rear. As he returned to evacuate another soldier, he was taken under fire by snipers, but raced beyond the friendly troops to attack and kill the snipers. After evacuating the wounded man, he returned to cover the deployment of the unit. His ammunition now exhausted, he dragged two more of his fallen comrades to the rear.[30]

Yet even A Company's attack failed: C Company, 2-27th's survivors were still trapped. With Meloy's mixed force pinned, and C Company isolated and surrounded, the initiative appeared firmly in the hand of Colonel Cam and the 101st PAVN Regiment. Another push would have certainly doomed the Americans. Meloy's two attempts to relieve C Company, 2-27th, had failed, and the situation appeared favourable for the 101st, despite a marked increase in American air support sorties and artillery fire on 4 November. However, help was on its way.

While everyone was focused on the main fight, Colonel Lynch and his mixed force with A Company, 2-1st, A Company, 4-31st and B Company, 1-27th had set off from his night laager as per De Saussure's instruction. Lynch was also joined by the CO of the 2-1st. Captain Garret's B Company, 1-27th, had made progress, but then De Saussure ordered it back. The force made little progress on 4 November. Yet the 101st had completely ignored these three companies while focusing on dealing with the ever-increasing force under Major Meloy. Control of the battle on 4 November had been less than effective. General de Saussure had focused his attention on Tay Ninh. During the night of 3-4 November, the 9th PLAF Division had launched its diversionary attacks against Tay Ninh and Suoi Cao. Tay Ninh had been mortared. While casualties were negligible, the communications infrastructure of the 196th Infantry Brigade suffered extensive damage.[31] The attack of the 272nd PLAF Regiment at Suoi Cao was repulsed, but it was a close-run affair requiring extensive air and artillery support on the Allies' part. Thus De Saussure's attention was diverted elsewhere at a critical moment.

On the morning of 5 November, Captain Garrett announced to the battalion commanders of the 2-1st and 4-31st that he was moving westward to the sound of the guns, to reinforce his own battalion. Colonel Lynch followed suit. The force, comprising three companies and two battalion command groups, started moving, then the two command groups withdrew west, apparently on De Saussure's orders. Garrett pushed on, with A Company, 2-1st, and A Company, 4-31st, in tow. On his own initiative, Garrett formed a battalion-sized task force and reached a position north of Meloy's perimeter. He was able to link up with his commanding officer by radio, and the two organised artillery support for an attack toward C Company, 2-27th.[32] Garrett's attack broke through the rear of the 101st PAVN Regiment. By noon, Garrett had reached C Company, suffering only a single casualty. Meloy instructed him to remove the wounded and continue east and then south, skirting the main enemy position and then joining the perimeter. By 1600 hours on 5 November, Garrett had reached the main perimeter. By then, Meloy had 11 infantry companies under his direct orders, more than a full brigade. The 101st Regiment had lost any remaining opportunity to overrun what was now termed

Task Force 1-27th. Meloy's ordeal was over, and with it Phase II of Operation ATTLEBORO.

Mike Forces to the front

While the 101st Regiment was engaging the bulk of the 196th Light Infantry Brigade and the 272nd attacked Suoi Cao, the ARVN III Corps and II FFV received intelligence of a possible two-regiment attack on Suoi Da. With the 196th engaged to the south of the Special Forces camp, III Corps decided to use the Mike Force battalion to conduct a combat reconnaissance to ascertain enemy intentions. On 2 November, Suoi Da was reinforced with Mike Forces units airlifted from Loc Ninh. During that same afternoon, the 3rd Company, call sign China Boy Three, was helicoptered to an LZ 10 miles north-east of the camp. Enemy forces were immediately contacted, requiring air strikes to cover the landing. Contact continued for the rest of the day and during the night, with the company continually supported by tactical air sorties. The next day, China Boy Three moved on foot to the north, while the 1st Company, China Boy One, landed on a new LZ south of China Boy Three's position. China Boy Three found an enemy fortified complex with bunkers and storage tunnels. They set out to destroy the complex, but while doing so were attacked by an estimated company-strength enemy force. With the help of nine air strikes, the attack was repulsed at the cost of three KIA, plus one US Special Forces and two Mike Force personnel wounded. Ten enemy bodies were recovered. During the evening of 3 November, China Boy One, the battalion's 1st Company, engaged an enemy platoon. The enemy was repulsed but at the cost of one USSF wounded.[33] As often in these actions, US Green Berets led from the front and suffered accordingly.

The following day, China Boy One continued patrols on foot but entered a minefield and suffered one killed and two wounded. A MEDEVAC helicopter was promptly dispatched, but it was downed by enemy fire with one additional KIA. China Boy Two, the 2nd Company, was helicoptered to the crash site to rescue the crew and protect the downed helicopter until it could be evacuated.

China Boy Three entered the camp that they had discovered the previous day to complete its destruction, but this time the position was defended. Enemy fire forced the company to break contact and withdraw again, but this time the enemy pursued. The Mike Force company was subjected to heavy small arms and mortar fire, despite receiving several air strikes in support. China Boy Three was in contact the whole afternoon but managed to receive a resupply via helicopter around 1900 hours during an apparent lull in the battle. The enemy then launched a determined attack, possibly with a full battalion. The attack force got to within grenade range, but China Boy Three managed to hold its positions, inflicting at least 50 casualties on their opponents. The unidentified Viet Cong unit withdrew when darkness fell. The enemy then put China Boy Three under siege for the whole night. Artillery fire and airstrikes were called in support. Beside night strikes delivered by F-100 and F-5 fighters, three AC-47 Spooky gunships were called in to provide flare support and direct fire. The three AC-47s expended 17,200 rounds of 7.62mm ammunition.[34] China Boy Three planned a breakout at dawn to establish a new LZ for resupply away from enemy positions.

However, the enemy pre-empted this by attacking at first light. The FAC orbiting over the night position immediately brought in two flights of F-100 Super Sabres, followed by one of B-57s. At 0730 hours on 4 November, Sergeant First Class Heap, the ranking USSF member of the company, was hit and informed the FAC of the situation: "I'm hit! All the Americans are either dead or wounded. We're being overrun!"[35] Contact with the company was lost for 90 minutes. With the FAC unable to determine the situation on the ground, two helicopter gunships approached the area at low level. Both were repeatedly hit. They survived, but reported the enemy was using smoke grenades to lure helicopters into flak traps. At 0900 hours, contact was finally re-established. The company, down to 80 effectives, had withdrawn to a position 1,300 metres south-west of the original perimeter and established a landing zone. Sergeant Heap lost consciousness several times but made it to the LZ with an ethnic Chinese Nung. Another Green Beret, Sergeant Hunt, was protected nearby by another Nung. MEDEVAC helicopters arrived and evacuated the wounded, leaving a new radio with the company. However, the Nungs only spoke Chinese, and none of the FACs airborne could understand them, let alone answer. A Nung officer was flown to take temporary command of China Boy Three and led the company to a link up with China Boy One and Two. The battalion-size force was airlifted back to Suoi Da on the afternoon of 4 November. The three-day action cost the force 39 KIA, 30 wounded and 44 missing in action. In addition, one Green Beret was killed and three wounded. By body count, 149 enemies were killed, with another 345 considered as possible kills, mainly from the air.[36]

6
ATTLEBORO: DEPUY TAKES COMMAND

General DePuy had been monitoring the whole operation from the start. Even if he never openly admitted it, he had his reservations about De Saussure. On 4 November, DePuy had arrived at the 196th Infantry Brigade forward command post at Dau Tieng, accompanied by one of the 1st Division assistant commanders, Brigadier General James R. Hollingsworth. De Saussure was at Tay Ninh, surveying the damage sustained in the mortar attack. At Dau Tieng, the brigade's staff appeared confused and unable to properly answer DePuy's pressing questions. Looking at situation maps, units' locations and brigade plans, DePuy, in the words of US Army historian George McGarrigle, "sensed a disaster in the making", sharing the same fear Major Meloy had on 2 November.[1] The difference was that DePuy had two stars, and immediately set out to address the perceived shortcomings. His first action was to order De Saussure back from Tay Ninh. When the 196th commander arrived at Dau Tieng, the situation did not improve as his personal maps showed different unit locations compared to the maps the brigade staff were using. DePuy completely lost confidence in De Saussure's plans for the following day.[2] DePuy offered advice and suggestions, and then left Dau Tieng with Hollingsworth. On the afternoon of 4 November, MACV Deputy Commander Lieutenant General John A. Heintges also visited De Saussure at Dau Tieng, and he too left unimpressed with what he saw. He flew on to Bien Hoa and asked General Weyand to meet him at the airbase. There, Heintges expressed his doubts about the state of ATTLEBORO and

General DePuy (on the right) taking over ATTLEBORO. (US Army)

6 November 1966, despite being already wounded, Major Guy S. Meloy (right) refused evacuation and continued to direct the fight at Dau Tieng without help from the 196th Infantry Brigade staff. (AP/25th Infantry Division Museum)

urged Weyand to transfer operational command and control of the operation to DePuy and his experienced 1st Infantry Division. Weyand concurred and issued the relevant orders.

After being placed in control of ATTLEBORO, DePuy did not waste time. He moved the 2-18th Infantry by air to Dau Tieng to provide security for the position and form a ready reserve. Then he ordered artillery and the 1-4th Cavalry to travel by road to the Special Forces camp at Suoi Da, where they linked up with the headquarters of the 3rd Brigade, 1st Infantry Division, which had been lifted by helicopter. Finally, he turned his attention to De Saussure and the 196th Light Infantry Brigade. De Saussure was told to break contact, unscramble his companies and re-form his battalions. While De Saussure was planning that, DePuy put Major Meloy in command of the whole force assembled next to the Ha Bao stream. He also installed Brigadier General John R. Deane, another of the Big Red One assistant commanders, to supervise De Saussure and, in case the latter failed to follow DePuy's instructions, take over the 196th.

Deane flew to Meloy's command post on the morning of 5 November to ascertain the reality of the situation. What he found further eroded De Saussure's position. Meloy, now wounded, was controlling eight infantry companies from four different battalions. Captain Garret, with his three additional companies, had not yet reached the perimeter. DePuy made a surprise visit to Meloy during the afternoon to coordinate the withdrawal of Task Force 1-27th. The general was shocked at the mess De Saussure had created. He was also extremely unhappy with the situation Meloy described. De Saussure had not visited Meloy at all and had been out of radio contact for 48 hours. The only contact with the brigade was the early morning visit of 4 November by the 196th Brigade S4 officer. Even more startling was Meloy's revelation that he had received the reinforcing companies as if from thin air, with company commanders reporting on the radio net without prior warning. De Saussure was relived of command and the brigade was returned for the moment to its old commander, Colonel Conaty.

Relieving De Saussure ended the mismanagement of the 196th's resources but did not change Major Meloy's situation on the ground. DePuy was assembling a cordon with 1st Infantry Division units south of Meloy's position to screen the latter's tactical withdrawal, but Meloy still had to break contact. Five companies were still in contact, some within 20 metres of enemy positions. First, the major pulled back his six unengaged companies to the rear, where they were picked up by helicopters. Then he moved his engaged companies, one by one, toward the safe area created by the other six. The engaged companies moved under artillery cover, with barrages targeted on the moving company's starting lines. As Meloy explained after the war, he had artillery ready to fire on command. When the order to fire was given, the company was also ordered to pull back in the 70 seconds before impact. In a testament to the professionalism of US troops, the tricky manoeuvre was executed without casualties.[3]

By the evening of 5 November, Task Force 1-27th had broken contact with the enemy. The final casualty tally was 60 killed and 159 wounded. The majority of the losses had been suffered by the two battalions of the 27th Infantry Regiment. The 25th Infantry Division had paid the price of De Saussure's convoluted plans. Enemy losses were unknown at the time, as was the precise identity of the enemy forces, although Major Meloy was sure it was the 273rd Regiment rather than the 101st.[4] The battle had been a stand-off, but enemy losses were higher. Battlefield policing from 7 November onward and captured documents suggested losses in the order of 200 KIA and 700 wounded.[5] The 9th PLAF Division even mentioned a company of the 101st's 3rd Battalion running, without orders, and the whole battalion being dispersed and out of contact for six days. Obviously, the 9th Division also boasted about its success, claiming 600 American killed.[6] What mattered was that the 101st had failed in its mission to destroy Meloy's force, and indeed Cam's entire attack had been a failure. Cam consequently ordered a retreat to War Zone C bases for his whole division.

Phase III

Senior Colonel Cam was not to leave the area unscathed, with General DePuy determined to maul the PLAF division as much as possible. General Weyand at II FFV agreed with DePuy. Within two days, DePuy assembled two of his brigades in the area – the 2nd and 3rd – via helicopter and air transport. He also approached ATTLEBORO in a different manner than his now disgraced predecessor, placing his faith in speed and firepower. He also kept his battalions as coherent units, something he had always advocated since 1944. Beside his own resources, DePuy could also count on massive support from the II FFV and 7th Air Force. He moved the 2-16th Infantry to Dau Tieng together with A Company, 3-21st Infantry, the latter from Loc Ninh. ATTLEBORO was changing face. As General Frederick Weyand put it at the time:

> Bill (Gen. DePuy) put a battalion in and then a reinforced brigade. He moved units all night and within 18 hours had the bulk of his division concentrated in the vicinity of Dau Tieng. I gave Bill an area and he started on search and destroys operations. It was fortunate he moved so fast. The 1st Division assisted the 196th get

straightened out. The 196th did a splendid job in getting the enemy to show his hand. The whole operation built up from the initial meeting engagement of the 196th. General Westmoreland directed the location of the 3rd Brigade, 4th Infantry Division [attached to the 25th Infantry Division]. The 173rd, with one of its battalions and two Vietnamese Ranger Battalions, was used initially to screen along the river in the eastern part of the area of operations and then sent into a search and destroy operation. The Sigma Teams took over the screening operations. The 25th Division on the left protected Bill's flank.[7]

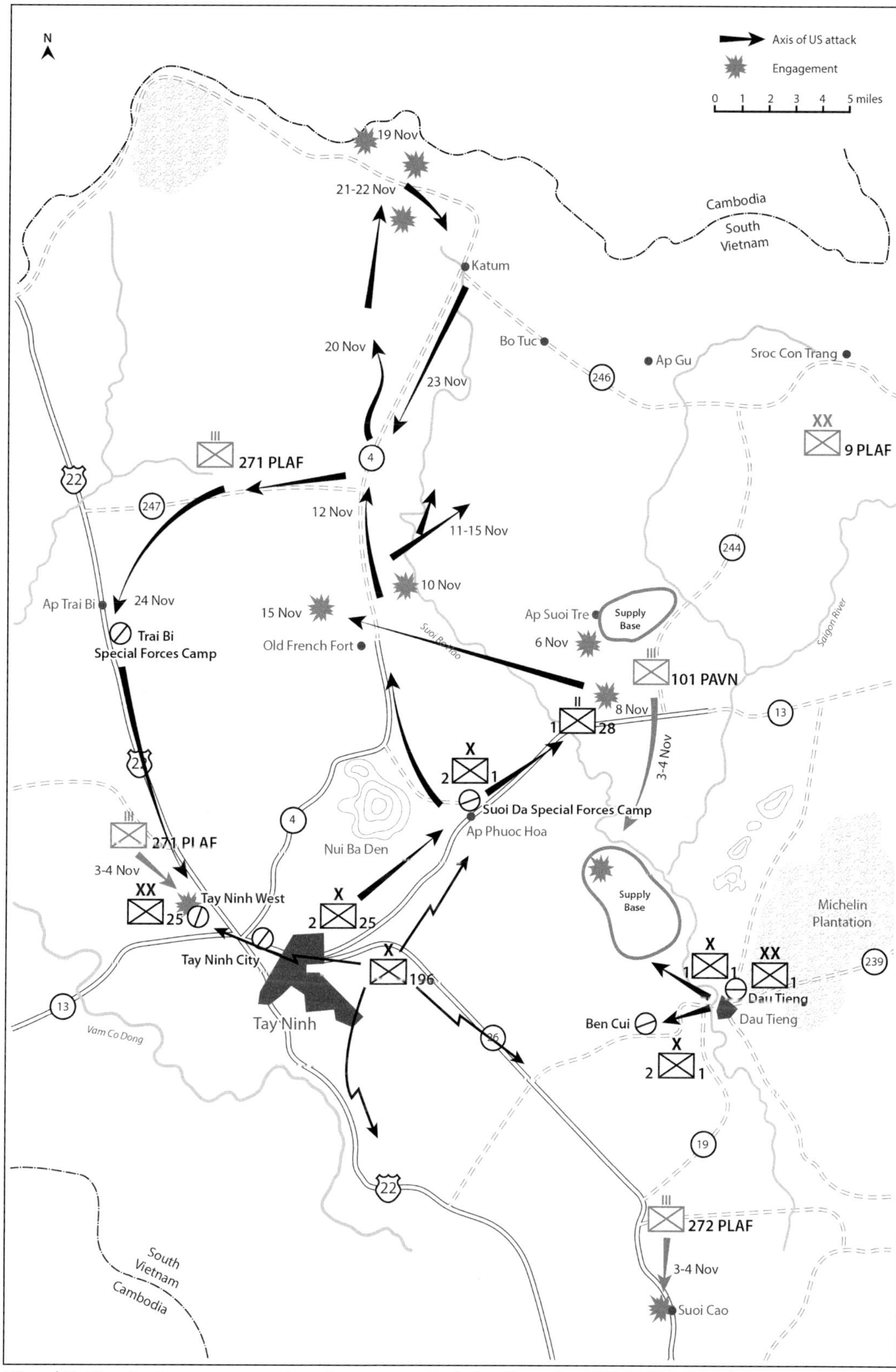

US and PLAF major troop movements and engagements during Operation ATTLEBORO. (Map by George Anderson)

On 6 November, ATTLEBORO became a full division operation, under DePuy and the 1st Infantry Division. DePuy initially renamed the operation BATTLE CREEK, to mark the change, but Weyand decided to keep the original name, so it remained ATTLEBORO. The 196th Light Infantry Brigade was now attached to the Big Red One, as were several battalions from the 25th Infantry Division. DePuy suspected that the enemy which the Mike Force had encountered between 2 and 5 November could have been elements of the same force Meloy engaged. He thus helicoptered two battalions 10km north of Meloy's battlefield, hoping to catch the elements that the Nungs had engaged or the retreating battalions of 101st Regiment. Mindful of the enemy forces, he also ordered each helicopter LZ be prepared with air and artillery strikes. On the night of 5-6 November, a helicopter belonging to the 25th Infantry Division had located motor convoys moving across the Cambodian border into South Vietnam. A Spooky gunship and several armed Hueys were dispatched. A mechanized infantry company with artillery support was also alerted. The ground force failed to make contact, but one of the helicopters reported ground fire. The following night, a US Army OV-1 Mohawk reconnaissance aircraft made a similar discovery, approximately 50km from the location of the previous incident. The convoy was moving with lights turned on. The Mohawk, call sign Hawk 09, reported moderate ground fire. An AC-47 and a flight of four F-100s were dispatched to deal with the convoy, with Army Huey gunships following. However, by the time the little air armada was in position, no lights could be seen or trucks spotted by the pilots.

While the USAF was hunting convoys, DePuy's troops made ground contact with the enemy. The 2-29th Infantry was airlifted close to the location where China Boy Three had been mauled and engaged enemy units almost immediately after landing. They were supported by F-100 strikes. Around 1.5km from the LZ, the 2-28th Infantry

8 November, Lieutenant Colonel Jack Witthed, 1-28th Infantry is calling air strikes on the positions of the PAVN 101st Infantry Regiment at Ap Cah Do. Note the exposed nature of his position and the radio antennas, tell-tale signs of a commander. At this point of the battle Witthed had already lost his three company commanders. (US Army)

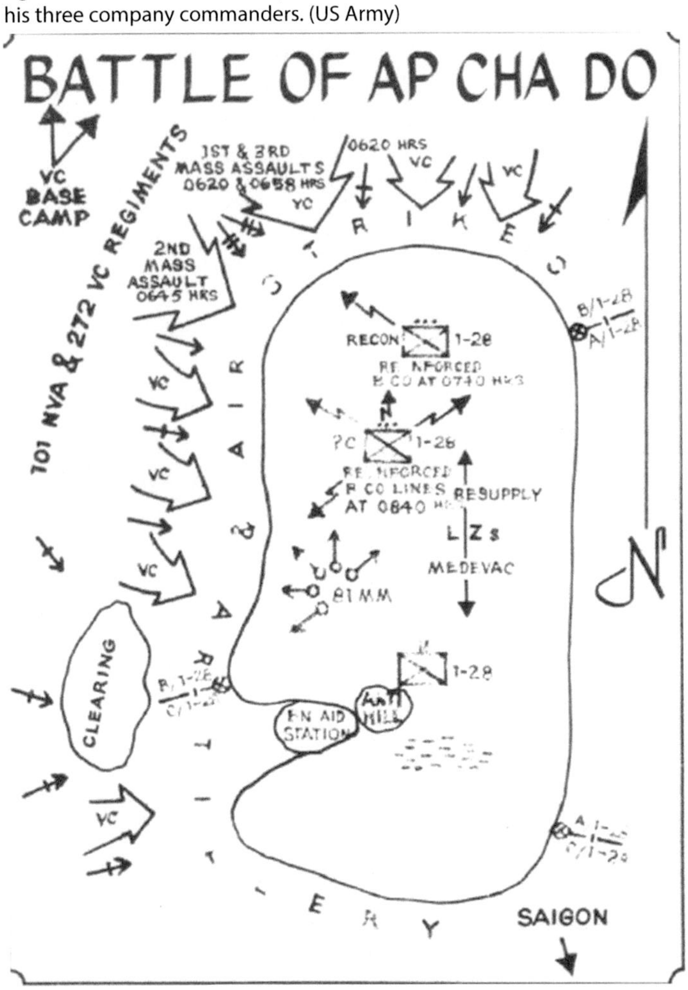

A sketch of the 1-28th Infantry position at Ap Cha Do and the enemy attacks made after the battle. Note the position of the battalion command post, and the fact that only 81mm mortars had been taken on operations. (US Army, sketch made by SP4 Henry Hunter)

assaulted another LZ following air and artillery strikes. Immediately after the 15 Hueys had landed the troops, the infantrymen reported receiving enemy fire from a densely wooded area. USAF Captain Ralph F. Wetzel, who was above the battlefield flying a FAC mission, later recalled:

Air support was critical for US operations. It was a quick way to exponentially increase the firepower of a unit in contact. During ATTLEBORO the majority of tactical sorties were performed by F-100D Super Sabres.

> Fortunately I had a pre-plan coming on station right at the same time. Silver (Silver-51) showed up and was just overhead as this mass of smoke started corning up. They were the first flight on this heavy concentration of automatic small arms fire.[8]

Captain Wetzel, following the directions of the command and control helicopter, began to put the strike on the largest concentration of fire:

> It was next to a tree line, but really all it was [was] a differentiation between a large canopy of trees and maybe a hundred feet beneath that, a shorter canopy of trees. There was a definite line there and a little break in [it] … [with] a .50-caliber in there … We put some bombs and napalm in there."

As the No. 3 in the flight was making his bomb run, Wetzel first noticed some .50-calibre tracer coming up from a position to the east of the original target: "I started to bring the flight on that position and all of a sudden the flight started seeing this. They saw flashes from 8,000 feet!"

The enemy had at least one heavy machine gun – either a .50 as Wetzel reported or a Soviet-made 14.5mm – and was using it in an anti-air role. The Super Sabre pilots in Silver 51 flight saw it and

An F-100D Super Sabre from the 481th TFS, 27th TFW from Cannon AFB – detached to Tan Son Nhut – performing a napalm attack. (Albert Grandolini)

tried to engage. The flight No. 2, Lieutenant Ken Backus, was hit, but later recalled:

> On the third pass I dropped a high-drag (bomb) as I was approaching the target. Over the target and pulling off, I noticed heavy … red tracers crisscrossing in front of the aircraft and over the canopy. I called out to the rest of the flight, 'Silvers, watch it, we're getting heavy tracers from both sides.' … In the meantime … we went up to strafe … the tree line where the heaviest ground fire seemed to be coming from. We had each made one strafe pass and I was on my second, (in) a 30-degree dive (at) between 450 and 500 knots, just walking it (the 20mm) right, down the tree line. As I started to pull off, the fire warning light came on … I pulled off and turned to the right where I knew friendly troops were and somebody started screaming 'You're on fire! You're on fire! You're trailing heavy smoke.'

Lieutenant Backus pulled away from the battle area and tried to head toward Tay Ninh. His F-100 was damaged but still flyable. When Backus was at around 5,000ft, the fire light went off, but at the same time his flight controls became less and less responsive. Then the F-100 went into a roll and the controls froze. Backus ejected. While still in the air, he realised there were three helicopters circling his position so he contacted them. Two fighters had already been deployed on CAP. At the same time, General Deane was flying over the battlefield in his command and control UH-1B. He saw the F-100 being hit and going into its terminal roll. Deane recalled:

> I saw the 'chute and circled this kid, until he got on the ground. The minute he hit, I hit the ground beside him with my helicopter. He jumped right aboard and we pulled him out. We like to take care of these boys who are supporting us.

On the ground, the 2-28th was still in heavy contact. Captain Wetzel continued to put strikes on the enemy positions until he was relieved by Captain Phillips. Phillips continued to direct strikes from his own O-1 until the late afternoon, when Wetzel's O-1 reappeared. The two FACs called in more than a dozen airstrikes. By nightfall, all three battalions – the 1-18th, 2-29th and 2-28th Infantry – were in contact. Air and artillery strikes continued throughout the night. A patrol from the 3rd Brigade, now settled at Suoi Da Special Forces Camp, located an enemy column before dark on a trail leading to Route Coloniale 13, north of Dau Tieng. The patrol immediately called in artillery and mortar support and added its own Claymore mines to the fray. The next morning, a reconnaissance of the ambush site revealed 70 bodies. DePuy's battalions had been able to keep contact with the 9th Division. At daybreak, the three battalions started to advance, uncovering shattered bunkers, abandoned camps, supplies and bodies. DePuy had started his own part of ATTLEBORO with a bang, with 170 enemy bodies recovered compared to only one US KIA and 23 wounded.[9]

The following day, the 9th PLAF Division tried to break contact. Yet it was clear that DePuy had made a major discovery, so Weyand decided to also throw the 25th Division into the fray, ordering O'Connor to deploy the division's 2nd Brigade to Tay Ninh to coordinate operations from there. After the brigade HQ was set up, Weyand ordered DePuy to switch back the three battalions he had on

The final component of American airpower were the might B-52s, either D or F versions, flying from Guam. These sorties were strictly controlled by SAC and the Secretary of Defense and required extensive planning. This made their use in tactical operations difficult and controversial. Often sorties were over the target area long after enemy troops had vacated. Later on, General Westmoreland obtained authority to change targets for the big bombers when they were already in flight, making targeting more effective. Here a B-52D is making a bomb run. (Douglas Pike Photograph Collection, The Vietnam Center and Sam Johnson Vietnam Archive, Texas Tech University)

Even if B-52 sorties were slow the big bombers carried a lot of ordnance. Operating in three-aircraft cell formations, three B-52s were capable of turning an entire area to ashes and obliterating everything inside. If enemy troop concentrations were indeed in the target area the effect was usually devastating. (USAF)

loan from the 25th. Meloy's 1-27th Infantry, 2-27th Infantry and 1-5th Mechanized thus returned to the Tropic Lighting. At the same time, the 3rd Brigade of the 4th Infantry Division, controlled by the 25th, also moved north. Weyand wanted O'Connor to use his mechanized forces along Route 4 and push north toward the Cambodian border to cut the 9th Division's retreat route.

Meanwhile, DePuy pressed the enemy in the Suoi Da area. He inserted two new battalions by helicopter north-west of the Special Forces camp. On 7 November, there were no reported contacts but several more caches were discovered. The 9th Division appeared to have vanished. In light of this, DePuy ordered Lieutenant Colonel Jack G. Whitted to prepare his battalion, the 1-28th Infantry, for an airlift on the morning of 8 November. Whitted's battalion, one of the two deployed that day, had patrolled north-east of Soui Da, in the same area where China Boy Three had been overrun. The position Whitted had selected for the night of 7-8 November was close to the location of the previous fight. But if Whitted hoped for a routine extraction, the 101st PAVN Regiment had other plans.

At dawn on 8 November, outposts alerted Whitted of possible enemy movement on their front. With the battalion still occupying its night defensive positions, his infantrymen dug-in and his Claymore mines still in position, Whitted recalled his outposts and then ordered a reconnaissance by fire. The American fire sparked a lively reaction. Two flares ignited and enemy troops returned fire from the northern face of the perimeter. Twenty minutes, later the 2nd Battalion of the 101st Regiment moved forward, straight into the Claymore mines. The North Vietnamese soldiers fell back to their starting position, while Whitted immediately requested air and artillery support. The brigade artillery had begun to move, so no howitzers were able to answer the 1-28th's requests for 20 minutes, but a FAC was already in the air and he alerted flights from Bien Hoa airbase. Major Doyal L. Wyrick had been above the general area of the engagement from 0615 hours that morning. Whitted's request for support came at 0624 hours, and by 0629 hours, the first four F-100s from Bien Hoa were already airborne.[10] Help was on the way.

They fighter-bombers appeared on the scene immediately after the first attack had been beaten back. At the same time, Captain Wetzel arrived in his O-1 to support Major Wyrick. The two FACs started to direct the F-100s. Brigade artillery was also starting to come online. Air and artillery support were consequently ready for the second company-sized North Vietnamese assault. This time the 101st Regiment tried the north-western side of the 1-28th's perimeter. The attackers faced another onslaught of Claymores, the defenders having detonated only their outer rings of mines in the first attack, along with determined defensive fire, 105mm shells and bombs. Wetzel later said

An M113 from 2-22nd Infantry; the track of Lt. Pryor (on the right brandishing a machete). The battalion was part of the 4th Infantry Division but ended up in III CTZ in exchange for one of the battalions that the 25th Division had deployed in the Central Highlands. (Mike Carpentier through 2-22 Infantry Association)

> We put the bombs out 200 feet in the jungle, although that was within the envelope of hitting the friend[ly] lines. But they were landing in the jungle (and) the fragmentation wasn't going to get to the troops. We put napalm in a little closer, the CBU (cluster bomb units) a little closer than that, and the 20mm right in the tree line.[11]

Yet the 101st appeared undeterred and fed company after company in the meat grinder, including those of a second battalion. The attacking force was later identified as comprising one battalion of the 101st Regiment and one of the 272nd Regiment. The attack was poorly coordinated, with each company attacking individually and with around five minutes between each attack. According to captured documents, the 9th Division "missed the chance to destroy the enemy in the pocket of resistance because lack of determination".[12] The missed chance probably had more to do with Colonel Whitted's men and their support. Attacks continued for several hours, slowly engulfing the whole perimeter. Determination did not appear to be in short supply on either side.

The battle moved from the uncertain light of dawn to full daylight. Wyrick and Wetzel were able to direct airstrikes more accurately, but daylight also allowed the enemy to target Whitted's officers. The radio antenna located close to each company command post and next to the battalion command group became inviting targets for enemy snipers. All company commanders and Whitted himself were hit. The embattled battalion commander stayed in the fight despite bleeding and was able to arrange replacement. Then, as often in battles, came a moment when personal initiative turned the tide. One of the replacement company commanders, Captain Euripides Rubio, realised that a smoke grenade intended to mark an enemy position for an airstrike was too close to his own company. He ran to the grenade to throw it into the enemy lines, was hit once and wounded but, undeterred, continued until he was 20 metres from the enemy. He then threw the grenade, being mortally hit at the same time. Captain Rubio received a posthumous Congressional Medal of Honor for his actions on 8 November.

Whitted also reinforced Rubio's men with the remaining elements of the battalion reconnaissance platoon, his last reserve. Hit by the airstrike Rubio had been instrumental in directing and several others, the enemy formation dissolved. The 101st had, for the moment, ceased to exist as a military formation. By 1130 hours, Whitted's men had cleared the last of the snipers from the trees and were free to police the battlefield. In total, 305 enemy bodies were discovered, while 85 more would be discovered in a tunnel on 9 November. The 9th Division claimed that "one [US] company has been completely destroyed [and] another suffered heavy losses (over two hundred men)".[13] In fact, the 1-28th had suffered only 19 KIA.

Whitted's action on 8 November persuaded DePuy that the enemy force close to Suoi Da was large and that he required more troops to deal with it. He asked Weyand for permission to deploy his own 1st Brigade. He was so uneasy with De Saussure that he did not want the 196th Brigade under his command. Weyand agreed. Westmoreland was also critical of De Saussure. Later, in his memoirs, the general would claim that De Saussure had employed his brigade piecemeal, and on the first significant action he had lost control of the 196th. Yet he also conceded that the circumstances were "rough" and possibly no one "could have done better" and accepted his own responsibility for De Saussure's appointment.[14] With the commitment of the 1st Brigade, DePuy had now deployed eight of his own infantry battalions, leaving only one to protect his division base. He continued to hound the enemy with the 2nd and 3rd Brigades, while the newly committed 1st Brigade protected the forward base at Dau Tieng. The two pursuing brigades continued to uncover enemy base camps and recover or destroy supplies. However, after the 8 November battle, neither the 101st nor the 272nd Regiments could be found.

While hunting for the retreating enemy, the 2nd Brigade took the opportunity to conduct a cordon and search operation at the hamlet of Ben Cui II, inside the Ben Cui plantation. Cordon and search operations were designed to surround villages with troops and perform both screening and civic action operations in the villages themselves. On 11 November, American troops surrounded the village, allowing Vietnamese National Police elements to conduct a search and to question its denizens. Unsurprisingly, most of the inhabitants were women, elderly or children. Few males of military age were found. At the same time, RVN officials organised a fair with music, food distribution and political speeches. More importantly, a US MEDCAP (Medical Civic Action Program) team treated 190 villagers. MEDCAP was often a more tangible form of persuasion than government fairs. The operation proved useful, with intelligence collected about the activities of the 82nd Rear Service Group, which used Ben Cui II as a collection point. Local villagers were used as purchasing agents for food and supplies in nearby Dau Tieng, then PLAF or PAVN troops would collect the products from the village.

The 2nd Brigade's information would help the 1st Brigade to uncover six large depots in the following days.

While the 1st Division tried to regain contact with the 101st PAVN and 272nd PLAF Regiments with fast helicopter raids, General Weyand instructed O'Connor and the 25th Division to locate the missing 271st Regiment north of Tay Ninh. Weyand and O'Connor relied on mechanized forces rather than helicopters. With the bulk of the II FFV helicopters supporting DePuy, Weyand decided to rely on Route 4 for both movement and supplies. With the 196th Light Infantry Brigade back under division control, O'Connor put its battalions on Route 4 between Tay Ninh and an old French fort at Bau Co. Located 10km north of Nui Ba Den mountain, the dominant geographical feature of War Zone C, Bau Co became an artillery firebase on 10 November. From there, O'Connor's guns could provide fire support along Route Coloniale 4 from Tay Ninh to the border. It was hoped that the 25th Infantry Division would not only locate the elusive 271st Regiment, but also trap the rest of the 9th PLAF Division.

7
RACE TO THE BORDER

Senior Colonel Hoang Cam was now in desperate straits. Not only had his brilliant offensive failed, but his division was in danger of being trapped and his supply network had been exposed. Even worse, he was losing control of his troops. Unbeknownst to him, the vaunted 9th PLAF Division was melting away. After the failure to take Suoi Cao and destroy Meloy's force north of Dau Tieng, Cam had reassessed his position. With the Americans literally sitting astride his supply area, he moved the 272nd Regiment northward, while ordering the 101st to protect the 82nd Rear Area Group. The PAVN regiment was sent to fight a rearguard action to delay DePuy's pursuit. It was supposed to screen the 82nd Group's depots or, at least, give time for their removal. The 101st was the freshest unit in the division at the start of the campaign, so was thus a logical choice for this mission. On the other hand, the regiment had been heavily engaged between 3 and 5 November and suffered accordingly. Its 3rd Battalion had seen one company running away in battle and the rest of the battalion dissolving, and not being able to reform until 11 November. The battalion commander was captured on 8 November. The 101st's attack on the 1-28th Infantry on 8 November was part of the rearguard action. But the collapse of the 101st Regiment completely unhinged Cam's retreat plan. The 82nd Group abandoned its depots and fled alongside the 101st.

Cam's division had been deprived of its supplies in a single stroke. Not only were DePuy's battalions methodically uncovering and destroying base camps, but without the 82nd Group, no one was left to deliver the remaining supplies to the 9th Division. On top of that, on 8 November, the first of a series of B-52 strikes was flown in support of Operation ATTLEBORO. While the results of the 225 sorties the big bombers flew in support of ATTLEBORO were never clearly quantified, they certainly contributed to Cam's discomfiture, hitting several suspected command and logistic positions. MACV evaluation credited the B-52s with at least three successful strikes on COSVN Command posts on 10, 14 and 15 November. One of the COSVN Deputy Commanders, General Lu, was wounded. Even if these successes were exaggerated, constant strikes forced constant redeployments, further disrupting an already shaky support system. Colonel Cam attempted to regain the initiative by massing his 271st and 272nd Regiments, the former toward Tay Ninh and the latter toward Dau Tieng. Attacking the city and the key supply base could have forced DePuy to stop his pursuit. Both regiments attacked their targets, mainly with mortar fire, on the night of 11 November. While the attacks caused some damage and light losses, they were not enough to divert DePuy.

At the same time, Westmoreland and Weyand reassessed ATTLEBORO. Westmoreland was pleased with DePuy's efforts but was also thinking in the longer term. The MACV commander told Weyand to continue ATTLEBORO, but to prepare to move DePuy's units back to their base in around a week. Meanwhile, the 3rd Brigade, 4th Infantry Division, would be moved to Dau Tieng to replace the 1st Infantry Division and the 25th Infantry Division's missing brigade.

Brigadier General John R. Deane is checking the location of 1-18th Infantry patrols with the battalion's staff. The battalion was taking part in Operation ATTLEBORO. 18 November. (US Army)

A gun crew of Battery A, 2nd Bn, 33rd Arty, fire a 105mm howitzer against the enemy in support of the 1st Bn. (US Army)

DePuy, who planned to blast the enemy with B-52 strikes. In the 24 hours required to plan and execute them, he used artillery and tactical air attacks to keep the enemy in place: "Between bomb and shell bursts that continued throughout the night, Colonel Marks' men could hear enemy movement within the strike zone. Then came the big bombs, and all was quiet."[2] In the morning, patrols entered the blast area. They discovered a few bodies and the usual array of destroyed structures. Marks concluded that the enemy had escaped, but B-52 strikes often left few human remains behind. On the other hand, the 3rd Brigade found a large medical centre. Intelligence later concluded that this was the central hospital for War Zone C.

For his push north, O'Connor concentrated two mechanized battalions – the 1-5th and 2-22nd – three infantry battalions – the 1-27th, 2-27th and 1-14th – and two artillery battalions. The assault force was grouped under the division's 2nd Brigade, commanded by Colonel Thomas M. Tarpley. Behind them, the 196th Light Infantry Brigade was still securing Route 4. Tarpley began charging north on 15 November. Contrary to normal in Vietnam, the mechanized battalions led the advance. The operation did not result in enemy contact until 19 November. That morning, one of the mechanized companies engaged an entrenched enemy platoon supported by an infantry company. The enemy was from the 1st Battalion of the 70th PAVN Regiment, the protection unit for COSVN. The M113s lined up and charged, submerging the enemy positions in a hail of fire. The PAVN units scattered, and the rest of the 1st Battalion, deployed nearby, refused to engage the American mechanized force. Later in the day, another mechanized company hit a defensive position, supported by dug-in machine guns. An infantry company from the 271st PLAF Regiment was also dispatched post-haste to reinforce the position. The US troopers called for air and artillery support, but the enemy held its positions until dark and then withdrew. Other reinforcing units, from the 1st and 2nd Battalions of the 271st Regiment, declined to fight despite being ordered to counterattack the Americans. The 9th Division units were not even responding to orders; the entire formation was collapsing.

The engagements on 19 November brought Colonel Tarpley an important gift in the form of fresh intelligence. Captured enemy documents revealed the location of the elusive 271st and of several elements of the COSVN infrastructure. Consequently, Tarpley brought all his five battalions forward and prepared for a showdown. But still the 271st, by intention or through fear, refused to fight. On 21 November, the 2nd Brigade command post came under mortar fire, but there were no further attacks. With the enemy refusing contact, Tarpley closed down his firebases on 22 November and began pulling his troops back to Tay Ninh. ATTLEBORO was coming to an end.

Westmoreland also approved Weyand's idea to push north toward the Cambodian border with the 25th Division. Not only did Weyand appear poised to cut the 9th Division's retreat path, but electronic intelligence had located several sections of the COSVN headquarters in the area about to be occupied by Weyand's men. The scene was set for the last act of ATTLEBORO.

With the 25th Division having shifted its efforts north, DePuy had moved his 3rd Brigade to Bau Co to continue searching the area. On 15 November, after intensive preparation from the air, Colonel Marks, the brigade commander, moved one of his battalions into a wooded area north-west of the French fort. After the battalion landed, Marks airlifted a second one. Each individual lift was made with just five helicopters due to the smallness of the LZ. This meant that the battalion arrived piecemeal. The third lift went in like the others and the troops landed, but when the helicopters took off and headed south, they suddenly flew into a "hail of enemy bullets".[1] Three Hueys were downed. Infantry already on the ground moved quickly to secure the crash site, rescuing the crews. Marks directed the battalion to continue landing but skirting the danger area. Once both battalions were on the ground, Marks ordered them to execute clover-leaf patrols to locate the enemy force. A clover-leaf patrol was a standard operation procedure: a company halted on the line of march, with each platoon entering an individual all-round defensive position and sending fire team or squad-size patrols to search adjacent areas following a looping route. According to the terrain, these patrols could range from 50–100 metres from the company line of march. Once they were in contact, Marks called a deluge of fire on the enemy positions. Under constant airstrikes, portions of the vegetation were cleared away, revealing an extensive base camp. Marks's men had found the enemy. With the onset of night, the two battalions dug-in in defensive positions and waited. Fighting continued during the night. The next day, a third battalion was helicoptered in. Marks's three battalions then attacked the base camp. The camp had been abandoned, but Marks's men found shattered fortifications, storage areas and several bodies. They also found an enemy unit, but simply pulled back and let the supporting arms do their gruelling work.

DePuy received electronic intelligence locating the 273rd Regiment north-west of Marks's battalions. The intelligence was accurate, even if the enemy unit was the battered 101st. It made no difference to

8
AFTERMATH

DePuy wanted another week to pursue the 9th Division, but Weyand was not convinced of the benefits. Cam's men, the ones still alive, had probably already crossed into Cambodia. He closed down ATTLEBORO on 25 November. On 29 November, Seaman returned to Bien Hoa and assumed command of II FFV again. He fully supported Weyand's earlier decision to shut down the operation. Back in Saigon, Westmoreland also concurred. The law of diminishing returns applied to ATTLEBORO. The 9th PLAF Division was nowhere to be found in Tay Ninh and Binh Long provinces. Senior Colonel Hoang Cam had indeed crossed the Cambodian border. The 72-day-long Operation ATTLEBORO, which started as a routine, battalion-size patrol involving a single separate brigade, ended as a multi-division offensive. To date, it was the largest allied operation of the war, a forerunner of things to come. At its peak, 18 US infantry battalions, three ARVN battalions and 24 artillery batteries were involved. MACV official reports claimed the operation had inflicted 1,106 VC/NVA KIA and 115 wounded, while 60 VC suspects were detained. These were numbers from the body count alone; MACV suspected artillery and air strikes had caused even more enemy losses. Furthermore, no one quantified PLAF and PAVN wounded. Considering the main hospital in War Zone C had been overrun by DePuy's 1st Infantry Division, it is not unconceivable that many of the wounded soldiers died from their wounds. According to MACV intelligence, four enemy battalion commanders had died in the operation, and at least one had been captured. Five company commanders had been killed or wounded. The same intelligence reports claimed enemy dead close to 3,000.[1] In addition to enemy casualties, massive amounts of supplies had been captured or destroyed. In return, US and allied forces suffered 155 KIA, 494 wounded, one aircraft and two trucks destroyed, plus one truck damaged.[2] The USAF and VNAF had flown 1,708 tactical sorties, 225 B-52 sorties and 3,314 tactical lift sorties in support of the operation.[3] By all accounts, ATTLEBORO was a massive effort crowned by success.

At its conclusion, US units returned to their bases, while Cam and his 9th Division coalesced in Cambodia, licking their wounds. Business in Tay Ninh and Loc Ninh provinces returned to normal. With the bulk of the fighting happening away from populated locales, it was as though ATTLEBORO had not even happened, despite the tremendous ordnance expended. As often in the Vietnam War, both sides claimed victory. MACV claims have already been discussed. Hanoi international broadcasts, meanwhile, claimed that "during Operation ATTLEBORO, 3,200 [US troops] were wiped out, the US 196th Light Infantry Brigade was put out of action and its commander, who was also commander of the operation, Brigadier General de Saussure, was relieved of his post, 52 aircraft were downed, and 55 military vehicles destroyed". The 9th Division history also described the whole battle as a "resounding victory".[4] In light of the facts, it is difficult to align the claims from both sides.

As usual, Hanoi's communiqués contained a lot of hyperbole and several factual errors. While De Saussure was relieved, he was not the commander of the whole operation. As for the numbers of casualties inflicted, they were simply unrealistic. The 196th was not put out of action; indeed its battalions remained in action for the whole 72 days. On the other hand, enemy losses reported by MACV could also have been inflated. There was some disagreement too between the various US commanders involved. For example, DePuy claimed all three regiments of the 9th Division, plus the 101st, had suffered heavy losses. MACV in Saigon was less sanguine. Subsequent captured documents painted a different image. The 101st Regiment had been severely mauled and the 272nd suffered significant losses, but the 271st had only been slightly engaged and the 273rd had not been engaged at all. Thus, enemy losses were not as high as DePuy believed. On the other hand, the performance of the 273rd and 271st could indicate they were much less combat-effective than the 9th Division's historians and Hanoi's broadcasters wanted people to believe. The 272nd's poor conduct could also be a symptom of the constant beating it had suffered during the previous year. American numbers were based on the body count system that, while not perfect, was much more accurate than some authors have claimed. MACV also collated information from a wide range of available intelligence, including captured documents, as the reduction of DePuy's initial assessment shows. Still on the numbers game, MACV also had something else to show: captured and destroyed equipment. ATTLEBORO netted 2,400 tons of rice, over 24,000 grenades, 600 mines and 2,000 pounds of explosives. Furthermore, 68 enemy base camps had been discovered and destroyed.[5] For a supposed resounding victory, the 9th PLAF Division had paid a heavy price (see Table 1).

Besides bean-, or in this case rice-counting, there were also other factors affecting the final value of the operation. For instance, what were the objectives, and were they achieved? The 9th PLAF Division had started the campaign with an offensive mission. Colonel Cam had been ordered to:

> destroy a vital element of the enemy, support the local movement, oppose [the] enemy pacification and expansion effort, break the oppressive government control, widen friendly liberated areas, and provide security and protection for storage facilities and base areas of Dung Minh Chau.

Seen through the lenses of COSVN's and B2 Front's orders, the battle had been a failure. Not one of the stated objectives had been achieved. No major allied formation had been destroyed, despite claims to the contrary. Enemy pacification was not opposed; the battles had been waged away from population centres and had not affected pacification at all. When Weyand decided that the 9th Division had been punished enough, his troops simply returned to their duty. Cam also spectacularly failed to provide security for base areas, as the materiel counts show.

On the other hand, US troops had pinned the 9th PLAF Division and its attached forces away from populated areas and subjected it to unrestrained application of firepower, with predictable effects. No GVN position had been lost. Enemy base areas had been ravaged, and not only had supplies been destroyed, but documents (123lb of them) were recovered, contributing to improve the MACV intelligence picture. Even if the 9th Division's losses were less severe than DePuy assumed, the division had been mauled. Furthermore, while on a tactical level the 9th Division had initiated the majority of the encounters, on an operational level, II FFV had retained the initiative. De Saussure's patrols had forced Cam to amend his plans and focus on reacting to American movements rather than fulfilling his own plans.

Table 1: Operation ATTLEBORO, Summary[6]		
Friendly Losses		
• personnel	115 KIA	494 WIA
• material	1 aircraft, 2 trucks destroyed	1 truck damaged
Enemy Losses		
• personnel	1,106 VC/NVA KIA (body count)	60 suspects detained
• material	300 buildings, 502 bunkers, 92 tunnels, 1 rice silo, 9 base camps, 1 claymore factory, 37 caves, 1 bridge, 12 sampans, 25 oxcarts destroyed	
	1,566 rounds small arms ammo, 4 M79 rounds, 33 60mm mortar rounds, 1 81mm mortar round, 5 105mm rounds, 2 155mm rounds, 117 grenades, 15 rifles grenades, 3 claymore mines, 12 anti-tank mines, 15 anti-personnel mines, 49 booby traps, 10-gal can TNT, 6 1-lb blocks TNT, 2 blasting caps, 55 CBU, 5 20-lb bombs, 1 100-lb bomb, 2 250-lb bombs, 4 500-lb bombs destroyed	128 small arms, 19 crew-served weapons, 2 M79 grenade launchers, 1 flare pistol, 1 50-cal MG barrel, 2 12.7mm hvy MG barrels, 5 hvy M mount/carriers, 5 bipods for 82mm mortar, 5,142 round small arms, 250 .50-cal rounds, 34 M79 rounds, 30 60mm rounds, 5 82mm mortar rounds, 9 RPG-2 rockets, 13 unk type rockets, 514 claymore mines, 12,288 hand grenades, 3,176 fragmentation grenades, 5,685 rifle grenades, 1,299 gas grenades, 825 large HE grenades, 2,000 WP grenades, 2 handmade grenades, 5 flares, 5 anti-tank mines, 6 anti-personnel mines, 11 floating water mines, 1,075 lbs explosives, 1,000 blasting caps, 3,000 booby trap igniters, 752 bangalore torpedoes, 500 fusing devices, 80 grenade launchers, 500 rifle grenade adapters, 400 claymore mine stands captured
	1,263.4 tonnes of rice, 800lbs of wheat, 7,955lbs of fish, 40lg bags fish, 11.4 tonnes salt, 250lbs canned food, 45 cans USC-rations, 35 chickens/ducks, 1 tonne beans destroyed	1,121 tons rice, 15 tons peanuts, 600 gallons cooking oil captured
	1,050lbs fertilizer, 460lbs clothing, 8 5-lb bags cement, 440gal tar, 500 gal gasoline, 30 gal kerosene, 9,000lbs tobacco, 50 picks, 61 shovels, 11 bicycles, 1 outboardmotor, 10 beds destroyed	123 lbs documents, 1 CW radio, 1 radio transmitter, 1 port[able] military radio, 3 transistor radios captured
	5 storehouses, 2 trucks, 1 rice processor, 1 55-gal drum C/S, 176gals acid, 2 arc welders, 23 rifle-stocks, 1 set scales, 1 rice mill, 2 tool boxes, 400 feet of electric wire, 1 air pump, 4 water buffalo destroyed	1 sampan engine; 1 bugle, 1,500 ammo pouches, 500 back packs, 151 bicycles, 2 tons corr[ugated] sheet metal, 68 bolts cloth, 50 bottles medicine; 380 vials of medicine, 1,000 unk type pills, 15 lbs sulfa drugs, 150 lbs Epsom salts, 2 lbs misc medical supplies, 1 large medical kit, 33 110-lb bags cement, 125 lbs clothing, 200 Pioneer tools, 98 batteries, 330 shovels, 10 green uniforms, 6 medical uniforms, 150 .lbs soap, 1,040 meters WD-1 wire, 160 gals POL, 2 crosscut saws, 321 machetes, 1 VC flag, 1 chemical agent treatment kit, 1-ton trailer, 4 gas masks, 1 farm tractor, 1 pig, 1 set scales, 1 pair binoculars, 2 refrigerators, assorted-machine parts/tools, 29 motorcycle tires, 10 inner tubes, 125 gals tar,· 45 qts paint, 8 tire rims, misc motorcycle parts captured

ATTLEBORO thus ended when General Weyand was satisfied with its results, not because Colonel Cam disrupted it.

At an operational level, despite some difficult moments, the Americans had retained the initiative for the whole operation. Adding these elements together, ATTLEBORO was a clear and significant American victory. II FFV dominated the area and forced its will on the enemy. Also, every engagement, even if initiated by the enemy, had its pace set by the Americans. There are several key elements that need to be discussed further. The American ability to react to contact was infinitely superior to that of the PAVN/PLAF. In no instance during the entire operation had significant PAVN/PLAF reserves been able to rush to a specific spot. Engaged formations had to count on their own resources. Once Colonel Cam had allocated his regimental task forces, nothing else could be done to help them. At an operational level, all formations were outside supporting range. At the tactical level, the PAVN/PLAF lacked the flexibility to deploy reinforcements and lacked coordination between different elements. On the other hand, US troops reacted quickly and were able to swiftly integrate themselves on the ground. Major Meloy's provisional 'brigade' was an example of this, as was Captain Garrett's battalion-size task force. The fighting between 3 and 5 November had plenty of common points with the more celebrated battle of la Drang. Flexibility and the ability to quickly concentrate reinforcements turned the tide in what should have been a PAVN attack with overwhelming odds. However, De Saussure did not show the same ability as the 1st Cavalry Division chain of command in managing the action. Yet from a tactical and operational perspective, US tactics, equipment, leadership and training were vindicated. On top of that, US operational approaches

Maj. Jack D. Watson, 1-18th Inf, 1st Inf. Div., keeps radio contact with the recon platoon who have sighted an enemy patrol in the area during Operation ATTLEBORO. (US Army)

18 November: medics attend to a wounded infantryman from 1-18th Inf. He had been wounded in the engagement with the enemy patrol. Whilst the operation was winding down, casualties were still being suffered. (US Army)

A USAF F-100 conducts a close air support strike on suspected enemy positions in support of the 1-18th Infantry on 18 November 1965, toward the end of ATTLEBORO. (US Army)

Thanksgiving Day 1966, an M113 from the 2-22nd Infantry had hit a mine. Damage seems moderate. (Mike Carpentier through 2-22 Infantry Association)

were largely sound and properly aligned with strategic imperatives. Weyand and DePuy thwarted Cam without endangering the larger pacification mission.

At a higher level, the evaluation of ATTLEBORO is much less clear. II Field Force Vietnam had achieved an operational success, but how did this success translate into broader strategy? Was operational advantage translated into strategic success? In this regard, ATTLEBORO was not particularly decisive. For all practical purposes, it was a spoiling operation that, while frustrating COSVN goals, did not alter the strategic situation. American troops simply returned to their own activities, without the whole strategic situation in the III CTZ being significantly altered. The 9th PLAF Division was still at large, and there was no clear-cut way to measure success in pacification. Still, the whole point of the 9th Division's autumn offensive was to hamper pacification efforts, so it could be argued that these efforts were hurting the whole edifice of NLF activities. From an MACV perspective, ATTLEBORO had never been envisioned as a decisive operation. Westmoreland's hammer blows were still to fall. ATTLEBORO was just another effort at keeping the enemy off balance while MACV was preparing its own regional offensive. In that sense, ATTLEBORO was just another strategic draw. The war continued and both sides continued to escalate.

It is almost ironic that ATTLEBORO should have developed in a different way. The 101st PAVN Regiment should have mauled Major Meloy's force on 4 November. It is undeniable that De Saussure made serious mistakes. His concept of operations for 3 and 4 November was nothing short of a disaster. ATTLEBORO was his first real operation, and he failed the test. Notwithstanding the soundness of his ideas in October and his ability to quickly scramble reinforcements in support of Meloy's 1-27th Infantry, his inability to work through his battalions and battalion commanders and his tendency to order companies around were disastrous. While on the map he appeared to saturate the area, on the ground his forces were scattered in unsupported groups unable to fend for themselves, and then mingled in a sort of amorphous conglomeration. De Saussure thus set up a favourable situation for the 101st PAVN Regiment to exploit on 4 November. Only Major Meloy's firm leadership, supporting fire and the ability of the American company commanders to work together even without

The minefield was made of old US-made anti-tank mines. This specific mine was disarmed and then placed at the battalion mess' door. (Mike Carpentier, through 2-22 Infantry Association)

prior joint training saved the day. After 5 November, the 9th Division had no more such chances of success.

DePuy's arrival completely changed the tune of the battle. The operation not only expanded in size but picked up speed. He did not spend time mixing companies but used battalions to their fullest. The commitment of the 1st Infantry Division also brought more supporting arms to the fray. The same could be said about the 25th Infantry Division. It is also worth noting that in Phase III of ATTLEBORO, helicopters were not the only way to achieve speed and flexibility. The 25th Infantry Division exploited its mechanized elements to achieve several brilliant victories. In that sense, DePuy, O'Connor and Weyand brought with them a combined arms team, while De Saussure just relied on his infantrymen.

On the communist side, ATTLEBORO only demonstrated Colonel Cam's inability to conduct a main force unit's war. He had wasted hundreds of men for nothing. Planning had been abysmal: his initial plan was over-ambitious and implemented with worn-out troops. He also ignored the basic principles of war, using unsupported and uncoordinated groups. There was no flexibility in the 9th PLAF Division's planning, and no anticipation of possible enemy moves. When De Saussure's actions spoiled the original plan, Cam was quick to react and seize the opportunity to attempt to destroy Meloy's isolated force. He showed at least the ability to reassess his situation but had few tools in his hand with which to act, a consequence of his flawed planning. The 272nd Regiment's attack at Suoi Cao was useless. While we do not know what really had gone wrong, it is not a mere guess to assume the 272nd was simply too worn-out to perform offensive operations. The 101st acquitted itself reasonably well, but despite fighting from extensive fortifications, enjoying numerical superiority and exploiting De Saussure's mistakes, it was unable to accomplish its mission. At best, the 3-5 November battle was a draw, and a draw that advantaged the Americans from an operational perspective.

Furthermore, once engaged, Cam never seriously tried to divert the US 196th Brigade or 1st Infantry Division from his logistical areas. As McGarrigle points out, the failure to reinforce the 272nd at Suoi Cao or to divert allied attention to other areas robbed the 9th Division of any chance to overwhelm Major Meloy and his assorted companies before they, for all practical purposes, become a reinforced brigade. A more significant effort could have diverted De Saussure's reserves to the south, and also forced DePuy and O'Connor to commit forces there during Phase III, thereby reducing the effectiveness of the subsequent sweeps and making Meloy's position more difficult in the short term. Cam simply played straight into DePuy's hands, as he had done for months. Despite the suggestion that the 196th Brigade was targeted

The aftermath, a battle-weary soldier from the Big Red One. (US Army)

because it was 'easier' compared to the 1st Infantry Division, nothing was done to prevent DePuy's troops interfering. The final mistake was not considering possible interference from other American units. Cam underestimated US mobility, flexibility and ability to reinforce units under threat. In broader terms, he underestimated the whole US Army. He was no better than De Saussure in his command performance, but, unlike the former commander of the 196th Light Infantry Brigade, he managed to save his job.

It is worthwhile speculating on the reason of Cam's underestimation of his opponents. As discussed in Chapter 2, there was a basic lack of respect for American troops, either because of ideological imperatives or overconfidence on the part of PAVN commanders. On the other hand, the tendency of the whole North Vietnamese organisation to underestimate the Americans and embellish reporting could have played a role. Cam could have been both guilty of unrealistic reporting, but also their victim. In the latter case, Cam believed what his regimental and battalion commanders reported for a year and he really assumed that the 1st Infantry Division had been seriously weakened and American battalions were being made combat-ineffective in scores. The whole autumn offensive was then designed to capitalise on this 'success'. In this case, the anonymous PAVN analyst's unvarnished comment quoted in Chapter 2 on the reliability of PAVN/PLAF reporting is even more damning. Yet ATTLEBORO demonstrated that the PAVN and PLAF had not yet learned how to cope with American troops, and it was uncertain if they would ever find a way.

The Americans, by contrast, proved fast learners. De Saussure's conduct of the battle was lacking. Once ATTLEBORO was upgraded to a full brigade operation (Phase II), he appeared unable to control it. On 3 November, his plan was overly complicated and contained the recipe for disaster. It was a miniature version of Cam's approach. He separated his units in scores of small packages that were not mutually supporting. He also directly controlled companies, thereby reducing battalion commanders to mere spectators. Once the situation deteriorated, he compounded his error. His absence from the battlefield on 4 November was serious, as was his lack of contact with Major Meloy. Again, he simply bypassed his battalion commanders. A historian could see an influence of the Pentomic division, where battalions were removed from the force structure and brigade/regiment commanders directly controlled companies, but De Saussure had never commanded a Pentomic battlegroup. McGarrigle also hinted at De Saussure's manpower-intensive approach using scores of companies to literally bash the jungle, as opposed to DePuy's more firepower-intensive approach. Either way, it failed.

ATTLEBORO clearly vindicated DePuy's and Seaman's concepts, created during months of constant engagements with large enemy formations. Their handling of the 1st Infantry Division in a whole year of battles against the 9th PLAF Division was excellent, and DePuy's tactical approach produced the expected results. Not only had American infantry battalions been able to repel everything Colonel Cam hurled against them for months, but actions such as the battle of Ap Tau O and the counter-ambush along the Minh Than road had demonstrated that the enemy ability to routinely block relief columns along roads had come to an end. In that sense, ATTLEBORO was the precursor of the later, larger, operation in the III CTZ, especially JUNCTION CITY. The II FFV had found a way to grapple and maul enemy main force units in areas where unrestrained firepower could be brought to bear, in turn reducing their influence on pacification efforts. ATTLEBORO showed that the Americans had found an operational method to achieve their goals, while the PAVN and PLAF had not.

Bibliography

Andrade, D., 'Westmoreland was right: learning the wrong lessons from the Vietnam War', *Small Wars and Insurgencies*, 19(2) (2008), pp.145-181.

Birtle, A.J., *US Army Counterinsurgency and Contingency Operations Doctrine 1942–1976* (Washington: Centre of Military History United States Army, 2007).

Birtle, A.J., 'Persuasion and Coercion in Counterinsurgency Warfare', *Military Review* (July–August 2008), pp.45-53.

Birtle, A.J., 'PROVN, Westmoreland, and the Historians: a Reappraisal', *Journal of Military History* (72) (October 20087), pp.1213-1247.

Brownlee, R.L. & Mullen, W.J., *Changing an Army, The Oral History of General William E. DePuy* (Washington: US Army, 1987).

Cameron, B., *Canister On, Fire! Australian Tank Operations in Vietnam* (Vol. I) (Newport: Big Sky Publishing, 2012).

Carland, J.M., *Combat Operations: Stemming the Tide, May 1965 to October 1966* (Washington DC: United States Army, 2001).

CHECO, U.P., *Operation Attleboro* (1967).

Cosmas, G., *MACV, The Joint Command in the Years of Escalation, 1962–67* (Washington: Government Printing Office, 2006).

Duiker, W.J., *The Communist Road to Power in Vietnam* (Boulder, Colorado: Westview Press, 1981).

Hoffman, G.F. & Starry, D.A. (eds), *From Camp Colt to Desert Storm* (Lexington: University Press of Kentucky, 1999).

Hukee, B.E., *USAF and VNAF A-1 Skyraider Units of the Vietnam War* (Oxford: Osprey, 2013).

Lehrack, O.J., *The First Battle* (Haverton, PA: Casemate, 2004).

McGarrigle, G.L., *Combat Operation: Taking the Offensive, October 1966 to October 1967* (Washington DC: United States Army. 1998).

Meloy, G.S., 'Operation Attleboro: The Wolfhounds' Brave Stand', *Vietnam Magazine* (1997), pp.38-44.

Moyar, M., *Triumph Forsaken* (New York: Cambridge University Press, 2006)

Palazzo, A., *Australian Military Operations in Vietnam* (Canberra: Army History Unit, 2006).

Palmer, B., *The 25 Year War: America's Military Role in Vietnam* (New York: Da Capo Press, 1990).

Pike, D., *War, Peace and the Viet Cong* (Cambridge, MA: MIT Press, 1969).

Sorely, L., 'To Change a War: General Harold K. Johnson and the PROVN Study', *Parameters* (1998).

Stanton, S., *The Rise and Fall of An American Army* (New York: Ballantine Books, 1985).

Stanton, S.L., *Vietnam Order of Battle; A Complete Illustrated Reference to US Army Combat and Support forces in Vietnam 1961–1973* (Mechanicsburg: Stackpole Books, 2003).

Starry, D.A., *Mounted Combat in Vietnam* (Washington DC: Department of the Army, 2002).

Stewart, Richard W., *American Military History, Vol. 2* (Carlisle, PA: US Army, 2009).

Westmoreland, W.C., *A Soldier Reports* (Cambridge, MS: Da Capo Press, 1989).

Wilkins, W., *Grab Their Belts to Fight Them, The Viet Cong Big Unit War against the U.S., 1965–1966* (Annapolis: Naval Institute Press, 2011).

Notes

Introduction

1 Richard W. Stewart (2009), p.319.

2 Max Boot, 'The Lessons of a Quagmire', *The New York Times* (16 Nov 2003).

3 Andrade (2008), p.149.

Chapter 1

1 As a matter of fact, the Army Chiefs of Staff during Eisenhower's presidency were hostile to him. After Joseph Collins left the post, the next two incumbents were Matthew Ridgeway and Maxwell Taylor. Both were Airborne commanders, and both criticised Eisenhower for the misuse of airborne divisions in 1944 and 1945, especially Taylor.

2 Ap Bac has become a sort of myth surpassing its real significance, with writers often repeating Vann and Sheenan's account with little further investigation. Often depicted as a victory of a couple of VC companies against a whole ARVN division, in reality it saw two entrenched VC battalions facing off, and being defeated by, the equivalent of a reinforced regiment. There were issues in evidence, but it was neither a turning point nor 'evidence' the ARVN was a bad army. Neil Sheenan, 'A Bright Shining Lie', and David Toczeck, *The Battle of Ap Bac*, contain the usual version. Mark Moyar, *Triumph Forsaken*, and Viet Ha Mai, *Blood and Steel*, contain completely different descriptions. The latter book is worthwhile because the author was an ARVN armor officer whose M113 company was involved in the latter stages of the battle, and it also contains the account of then Captain Ba Ly Tong, who commanded the mechanized company engaged from the start.

3 Usually it is assumed that MACV was just an enlargement of MAAGV, yet it was technically a new organisation assuming control of MAAGV until the latter was dissolved. Cosmas (2006).

4 Letter Gen. Bruce Palmer to John Paul Vann, 14 Jan 1964, Vann papers MHI, quoted in Cosmas (2006), p.124.

5 Birtle, 'US Army Counterinsurgncy and Contigency Operations Doctrine 1942–1976' (2007).

6 Duiker, p.407.

7 Wilkins (2011), p.77.

8 Wilkins (2011), p.133.

9 Military History Institute of Vietnam, *The Saigon-Gia Dinh Offensive Theater (1968)*, p.87.

10 Quoted in Lehrack, p.45.

11 Wilkins (2011), p.216.

12 Wilkins (2011), p.128.

13 Lich Su, p.527.

14 Wilkins (2011), p.129.

15 Pike, pp.135-137.

16 Brownlee & Mullen (1987), pp.131-133.

17 Telegram, Commander, MACV, to Chairman, JCS, 30 June 1965, FRUS, June–December 1965, 76.

18 Andrade (2008), p.147.

19 Carland (2001), p.357.

20 McGarrigle (1998), pp.11-12.

21 Andrade (2008), p.156.

22 Andrade (2008), p.156.

23 Thompson, *No Exit from Vietnam*, p.133; Coates, quoted in Cameron (2012), p.44.

24 Sorely (1998), p.102.

25 Andrade (2008), p.158.

26 McGarrigle (1998), p.12.

Chapter 2

1 Available sources are confused as to the exact designation of the division's supporting units. For example, Wilkins identifies the 5th PLAF Division Reconnaissance Company as the 95th (Wilkins, *Grab their Belts*, p.103), but MACV put Reconnaissance Company 95 with the 9th (MACV, History of 273rd VC Regiment, 1970, p.12).

2 NVA officer quote from McCoy, *Secrets of the Viet Cong*, p.5.

3 Lanning and Cragg, *Inside the VC and the NVA*, p.128.

4 The term 'regrouped' Southerners indicate communist cadres and troops that moved north across the 17th Parallel after the 1954 Geneva Accords and were then infiltrated in South Vietnam after 1959.

5 Pham Quang Dinh, *Su Doan 9*, p.51.

6 *Su Doan 9*, pp.9-10.

7 'History of the 273 VC Regiment, July 1964–December 1969', Assistant Chief of Staff, G2 USARV (1970), p.4.

8 '273 VC Regiment', pp.4-6.

9 According to Wilkins, the claim is made in the official division history, *Su Doan 9*, p.49, but it is not supported by the biographical entry about Cam in the official Military Encyclopedia Center of the Ministry of Defence. Windrow's work on Dien Bien Phu does not mention the episode; Windrow, *The Last Valley*. Considering the unreliable nature of the 9th Division official history, the claim must be considered as suspicious at least.

10 McGarrigle (1998), p.35.

11 'Tay Ninh Campaign', pp.4-6, and *Su Doan 9*, pp.76-78.

Chapter 3

1 Cosmas, *MACV: The Years of Escalation 1962–1967*, p.244.

2 Cosmas (2006), p.398.

3 Stanton, *Rise and Fall of an American Army*, p.75.

4 4-31st History.

5 4-31st History.

6 William Westmoreland, *A Soldier Reports*, p.275.

7 Carland (2001), p.33.

8 Seaman to Albright, 10 September 1970, pp.6-10, quoted in Carland (2001), p.33.

9 S. Stanton (1985), p.22.

10 Starry (2002), pp.5-6.

11 Starry (2002), p.56.

12 Johnson to Westmoreland, 31 July 1965.

13 Brownlee & Mullen (1987), pp.93-94.

14 McGarrigle (1998), p.45.

15 Carland (2001), p.337.

16 'Evaluation of United States Army Mechanized and Armor Combat Operations in Vietnam' (1967). Usually referred as the 'MACOV Study or Report'. Started in 1966 and completed in 1967, it was a MACV-wide effort to learn from the actual use of tanks and armoured vehicles in country and develop lessons and recommendations. It prompted a positive reassessment on the utility of tanks and armoured vehicles.

17 Hukee (2013), p.11.

Chapter 4

1 Wilikins (2011), p.109.

2 Carland, p.79. The estimate came from General Williamson, the 173rd AB Commanding Officer, and was an estimate not based on any form of body count. Later MACV estimates increased enemy losses to 700, but that was far in excess of the 3rd Battalion, 271st Regiment's probable strength.

3 Hoffman & Starry (1999), p.325.

4 Starry (2002), pp.3-6.

5 Starry (2002), pp.54-56.

6 Carland (2001), p.87.

7 Annex C, AAR 3rd Bde, 1st Inf Div, Operation Bushmaster.

8 AAR 3rd Bde, 1st Inf Div, Operation Bushmaster, p.9.

9 Annex C, AAR 3rd Bde, 1st Inf Div, Operation Bushmaster.

10 Dinh, *Su Doan 9*, p.59.

11 AAR 3rd Bde, 1st Inf Div, Operation Bushmaster.

12 Carland (2001), p.88.

13 AAR OPN El PASO II/III, p.9.

14 The M132 was an M113 mounting a small turret equipped with a flamethrower.

15 General DePuy estimated enemy losses as 90% of the 1st Battalion and 50% of the 2nd; Carland (2001), p.313.

16 Dinh, *Su Doan 9*, p.71.

17 AAR OPN EL PASO II/III 1st Infantry Division.

18 The confirmed body count is confused for that action, ranging from 21 to 98, with some estimates in the order of 100-plus. US casualties were relatively low, with 13 KIA and five wounded; Carland (2001), p.319.

19 AAR OPN EL PASI II/III, p.48.

20 Carland (2001), p.325.

21 Dinh, *Su Doan 9*, p.180.

22 Dinh, *Su Doan 9*, p.74.

23 Dinh, *Su Doan 9*, pp.64-65.

24 Carland (2001), p.336.

Chapter 5

1 After Action Report, Tay Ninh Campaign (3 Nov–30 Dec 66), Military Affairs Committee (Group 129), SVN Liberation Army, No 23/N1 1 Feb 67, p.5; translated and included in Rpt MACV J-2 Log 03-3331-67.

2 After Action Report, Tay Ninh Campaign (3 Nov–30 Dec 66), Military Affairs Committee (Group 129), SVN Liberation Army, No 23/N1 1 Feb 67, p.5; translated and included in Rpt MACV J-2 Log 03-3331-67.

3 McGarrigle (1998), *Tay Ninh Campaign*.

4 Moyar (2006).

5 Harris, *Vietnam High Ground*.

6 196th IB Journal, 23 October 1966, 2358 entry.

7 McGarrigle (1998), p.37.

8 196th Light Infantry Brigade, Operation Attleboro AAR, 3 Nov 1966.

9 McGarrigle (1998), p.38.

10 Guy S. Meloy Interview, *Vietnam Magazine* (October 1997), pp.40-41

11 196th Light Inf Bde AAR, 3 Nov 1966.

12 Meloy (1997), p.41.

13 Meloy (1997), p.41.

14 Meloy (1997), p.41.

15 McGarrigle (1998), p.38.

16 McGarrigle (1998), p.38.

17 Meloy (1997), p.41. Note, General Meloy indicates Route 9, while McGarrigle says Route 19; McGarrigle (1998), p.40. Actually it was Route 19, an old French logging road.

18 McGarrigle (1998), p.40.

19 Meloy (1997), p.42.

20 AAR 2-27, p.4.

21 AAR 2-27, p.4.

22 Meloy (1997), p.42.

23 AAR 2-27, p.4.

24 Meloy (1997), p.40.

25 Meloy (1997), p.42.

26 AAR 2-27, p.4.

27 Meloy (1997), p.42.

28 Meloy (1997), p.43.

29 Captain Robert F. Foley Medal of Honor Citation.

30 Private First Class John F. Baker Jr Medal of Honor Citation.

31 McGarrigle (1998), p.38.

32 Meloy (1997), p.43.

33 USAF CHECO Report, Operation Attleboro, pp.8-9.

34 CHECO (1967), p.14.

35 CHECO (1967), p.14.

36 CHECO (1967), p.16.

Chapter 6

1 McGarrigle (1998), p.41; Meloy (1997), pp.40-41.

2 McGarrigle (1998), p.41, based on interview by McGarrigle with DePuy, 3 Oct 77.

3 Meloy (1997), p.43.

4 Meloy (1997), but the more recent work of McGarrigle, also using enemy documents, identifies the opponents as the 101st; McGarrigle (1998), pp.39-44.

5 McGarrigle (1998), p.44; the 9th Division admitted only 67 between KIA and wounded, *Tay Ninh Campaign*, p.9.

6 *Tay Ninh Campaign*, p. 9; McGarrigle (1998), p.44.

7 CHECO (1967), p.18.

8 CHECO (1967), pp.21-23; also the following excerpts.

9 After Action Report, Operation Battle Creek, 3rd Bde, 1st Inf Div, 15 Dec 1966, pp.3-4.

10 CHECO (1967), p.26.

11 CHECO (1967), p.26.

12 *Tay Ninh Campaign*, p.9.

13 *Tay Ninh Campaign*, p.9.

14 Westmoreland (1989), p.276.

Chapter 7

1 McGarrigle (1998), p.55.

2 McGarrigle (1998), p.55.

Chapter 8

1 Intell. Report, 149th MIGp, COMUSMACV (DD1396), 6-026-1943-66, dtd 14 Dec 66 (Doc 17).

2 Project CHECO, Operation Attleboro, p.41.

3 CHECO, Attleboro, p.41.

4 *Su Doan 9*, pp.75-78.

5 McGarrigle (1998), p.58.

6 From US MACV Daily Sitrep, pp. 328-66

ACKNOWLEDGEMENTS

This book is something that started when was still researching my PhD in King's College London. There my guide through the US military and modern warfare were Professor Brian Holden Reid and Philip Sabin. Without them I would not have reached the point to write a book on Vietnam. I want also t thank Colonel Robert Schexnayder and the 2-22 Historical Association, the staff at the McCormic Research Center of the 1st Infantry Division Museum, the Staff at National Archives and Record Administration, and the staff at the Tropic Lighting Museum who all helped in collecting imagery and material for the book despite the pandemic. Also both my editors have to be commended, Tom Cooper and Andy Miles at Helion for the support they provided in this project and for dealing with a slow moving Italian. Finally I want to dedicate this book to the person who started me on the road of Vietnam reseach, the late Professor Saki Ruth Dockrill.

ABOUT THE AUTHOR

Dr. Arrigo Velicogna is an academic historian, a conflict simulation designer and defence consultant specialized in military history, operations, and naval warfare. He earned a PhD in War Studies in King's College London in 2014 on the subject of the Vietnam War. He taught related subjects there and at Wolverhampton University, and worked for several British defence related organizations. *Into the Iron Triangle* is his first book for Helion.